*"let's
just be
friends"*

"let's just be friends"

recovering from a broken relationship

H. Norman Wright

Fleming H. Revell

A Division of Baker Book House Co
Grand Rapids, Michigan 49516

© 2002 by H. Norman Wright

Published by Fleming H. Revell
a division of Baker Book House Company
P.O. Box 6287, Grand Rapids, MI 49516-6287

Printed in the United States of America

Library of Congress Cataloging-in-Publication Data

Wright, H. Norman.
    Let's just be friends : recovering from a broken relationship /
H. Norman Wright.
       p.   cm.
    ISBN 0-8007-5803-X (pbk.)
    1. Man-woman relationships. 2. Separation (Psychology) I. Title.
HQ801 .W842 2002
306.7—dc21
                                              2002004088

Unless otherwise indicated Scripture is taken from the HOLY BIBLE, NEW INTERNATIONAL VERSION®. NIV®. Copyright © 1973, 1978, 1984 by International Bible Society. Used by permission of Zondervan. All rights reserved.

Scripture marked AMP is taken from the Amplified Bible, Old Testament. Copyright © 1965, 1987 by The Zondervan Corporation. Used by permission.

Scripture marked ICB is taken from the *International Children's Bible, New Century Version,* copyright © 1983, 1986, 1988 by Word Publishing, Dallas TX 75039. Used by permission.

For current information about all releases from Baker Book House, visit our web site:
http://www.bakerbooks.com

Contents

Part 3 Moving On

Introduction

You may be wondering if another book for singles is necessary. The answer is yes, and here's why. When people go through a breakup, they go through a tremendous amount of pain, yet their pain is often neglected. People who go through a divorce, on the other hand, have numerous resources available to help them, from books to videos to divorce recovery groups. Why should those who go through a breakup be left behind? The pain and emotional turmoil of a breakup is in many cases comparable to that of a divorce.

Hopefully this book will meet the need. Discovering how to recover from a broken relationship can reduce the pain, accelerate the healing process, turn the experience into one of learning and growth, and help people to be better equipped for a future relationship.

Throughout the book I will refer to friends and counselees by name. While these people are for the most part made up, they are realistic representations of the many individuals I have counseled through breakup experiences over the course of thirty-five years of professional counseling.

I've sensed a need for this book for years and many have requested it. My hope is that *"Let's Just Be Friends"* will speak to you, ease the pain, and support your recovery and growth.

Part 1

Ending a Relationship

1

Red Flags
Possible Reasons to End a Relationship

Many people are caught off guard when their relationships end. It seems as if everything is going fine one day, and the next day a conversation happens, a door slams, and it's over. But in actuality very few relationships deteriorate and end this quickly. The vast majority show signs of decline long before the breakup, and if you're aware of these, you'll be better prepared for the end of your relationship. I call these signs "red flags."

Red Flag #1: The Relationship Is Out of Balance

One type of relationship that is not likely to last very long is the "out of balance" relationship. This is when you and your partner do not care about each other equally. One of you may have pursued the other, and now the other wants to pull back. Or sometimes one person tries valiantly to feel lovingly toward the other, but it just doesn't work.

If you're currently in a relationship, you may think the difference between how you treat your partner and how your partner treats you is due to a difference in your personalities. This could be, but don't ignore the possibility that one of you simply doesn't care as much.

It's difficult to admit that you may care more for the other person than he or she cares for you. But if it's true, and you know it's true, don't deny it. Denying it will only cause more pain in the end.

Your relationship may be out of balance if you or your partner

initiates most of the contact for the relationship

initiates most of the affectionate advances such as holding hands, hugs, and kisses

is always the one who makes plans, while the other just seems to go along

sacrifices to do things for the other, but the sacrifices are not reciprocated

is excited about the relationship, while the other person seems merely to be along for the ride

receives a less-than-enthusiastic response when talking about future plans for the relationship

Red Flag #2: One of You Is a Rescuer

When I was in high school and college, some of my friends had summer jobs as lifeguards on the beaches and public pools. To me, lifeguarding was a dream job. These guys were in the sun all day, usually surrounded by kids their own age, and the hours were good. As summer came to an end, I'd say to them, "What a great summer job you had! I'll bet you're sorry it's over." Many of them surprised me, saying, "Not really. I'm tired of constantly rescuing people."

12

But when it comes to relationships, some people never tire of being rescuers. They live for it. In a healthy relationship, you want to be there for the other person and he or she wants to be there for you. That's the healthy way to relate. If you find you're the one who is always there for your partner, and he's like a ghost when you need him, you've got a problem. Is your partner there for you?

Sometimes the rescuer takes the initiative to save the other person. Other times the person in need of rescue will manipulate the rescuer to spring into action.

When someone is always rescuing another person, the person being rescued begins to learn that she does not need to change because her partner is always there to bail her out. And even though the motives of the rescuer may be noble, in time the message he sends is, "I'm better than you are, and you're not capable of handling things yourself." Eventually the person being rescued begins to resent the rescuer.

I've seen "rescuers" repeat this pattern with different partners. They're attracted to people who need them. If you think this is the case with you, think about the future of any relationship in which one person is always rescuing the other. Most of these relationships don't last, and if they do, they're terribly unhealthy. If you find yourself attracted only to people who are weak and needy, and if on the other hand you are turned off by people who have strong wills, you have some work to do.[1] Discovering the reason for this attraction and correcting this tendency are important things to do.

Red Flag #3: Your Relationship Is Built on Possibilities, Not Reality

Think back to the beginning of your relationship. Do you remember thinking your partner wasn't what you

13

wanted him to be, or what you had hoped for, yet you found yourself thinking, *He has so much potential!*

Perhaps he wasn't what you were looking for spiritually, but you thought, *The Lord could really do wonders with him!* Perhaps he seemed apathetic, but you thought, *Well, he's just waiting for the right opportunity to come along.*

Perhaps your partner's emotional outbursts were disturbing, but you thought, *I'll be able to help him get a handle on that anger and depression eventually.*

Perhaps you thought the way your partner eyed the opposite sex was just because you and he were not committed or married yet. You thought, *Once that happens, he'll only have eyes for me.*

Perhaps the way he handled his finances was a bit scary, especially with all those credit cards maxed out. But you thought, *I'm sure he'll learn responsibility once we're married.* In fact, didn't he offer to open a joint checking account and credit card with you so the two of you could learn to work closer together financially? That could have led you both to bankruptcy!

Perhaps he didn't communicate very much or share with you on an emotional level. But you rationalized, *Who would, coming out of that abusive, alcoholic, dysfunctional background?* You've met his parents and they were cases out of a mental health textbook. In time you expected to fill in all those gaps for your partner, thinking then he would be a whole person.

You made excuses for him. Perhaps the reason he jumped from relationship to relationship in the past was because no one had ever cared for him enough. You thought, *Getting him involved in my church and Bible study should make a difference.* Did it?

If you've built your relationship on all these possibilities, the problem was *not* the other person. You know who the problem was. Expecting to change another person fundamentally is as silly as expecting gold from a lead mine.

Red Flag #4: One of You Is a Perfectionist

In relationship terms, a perfectionist is someone who embarks on a crusade to "help others fulfill their potential." In order to prove he is good enough, the perfectionist strives to do what no one else can do. He sets unrealistic goals and sky-high standards for his relationship, and he sees no reason why he and his partner shouldn't achieve these standards. The couple strains to reach these goals; they're driven by "musts," "shoulds," "have to's," and "never good enough" thoughts. The perfectionist overschedules, overworks, overdoes, and comes unglued when surprises or unforeseen changes crop up. Soon the perfectionist is overwhelmed by the arduous tasks he has set for himself.

Expecting to change another person fundamentally is as silly as expecting gold from a lead mine.

The standards of a perfectionist are so high that no one could attain them consistently. They are beyond reach and reason. The strain of reaching them is continual, but the goals are impossible. Yet perfectionists believe their worth is determined by attaining these goals.

Because perfectionists live with the fear of failure, they often procrastinate. They take positive traits to the extreme and make them liabilities. Neatness, punctuality, responsibility, and attention to details are usually great things to have on board a relationship, but a perfectionist contaminates them. He makes them all-or-nothing requirements that only stifle the relationship.

A perfectionist has trouble finding an acceptable marriage partner and has difficulty forming relationships that lead to marriage. Perfectionists want perfect mates, not

15

human ones. Sometimes they reject potential partners, often delaying marriage for years.

A perfectionist often looks upon marriage as another achievement. A prospective mate may at first be viewed through rose-colored glasses and seen as "perfect." But the fantasy soon fades, especially after marriage. A friend of mine, Dr. Dave Stoop, describes the situation graphically when he says, "The spouse is no longer a prince or princess, but has turned into a project!" Now the focus of attention is on making the imperfect partner perfect!

I've seen married men and women who don't allow their partners to get to know them. They tend to retreat and live behind closed emotional doors. They're afraid they'll be found lacking in some way. Many a husband quietly accepts his perfectionist wife's demands that he not wear shoes in the living room because she is afraid he'll leave scuffs on her "perfect" carpet. He puts up with this, and not only does he feel uncomfortable in his own home, but also in time his feelings for his wife change.

Perfectionists have a "corrector" tendency. There is a right and perfect way to do everything. When a perfectionist's spouse is washing dishes, the perfectionist walks over and turns down the water because his spouse is using too much. Perfectionists rearrange the canned goods in the cupboard according to their system of efficiency. They make unsolicited comments about their partner's clothes with disclaimers like "I just want you to look your best and make a good impression."

When you're in a relationship with a perfectionist, it's easy to fall into the trap of blaming and berating yourself, walking on eggshells, or getting down on yourself when your perfectionist partner is offended by your constructive criticism.[2] Keep in mind that perfectionism is neither a spiritual gift nor a calling from the Lord. It's the way certain personalities choose to build their own security.

Red Flag #5: One of You Is a Controller

If you're with a controller, you're likely to feel the same pressure as you would with a perfectionist. Men and women use control to protect themselves from real or imagined concerns. Their use of control is part of their survival system. They believe that "the best defense is an offense," and the offensive strategy they employ is that of staying in control. They live in fear of the results and consequences of not being in control. They're afraid of rejection, abandonment, hurt, disappointment, and losing control itself. They may also be addicted to the respect, power, or emotional rush they get from controlling others.

Controllers use a variety of methods to get their partners to do what they want. Both controllers and perfectionists use absolutes such as *always* and *never.* They fail to give their partners the benefit of the doubt. They use phrases like "If it weren't for you . . ." or "Because of you I . . ." These are *blame* and *shame* statements. Responsibility for whatever has gone wrong in the controller's life is thrust onto another's shoulders, whether valid or not.

Controllers are clever. They often *shift the blame* to get their point across. In this way they don't have to shoulder any responsibility themselves.

Red Flag #6: One or Both of You Is Consumed with Anger

Another relationship problem is when one or both of the members of a couple are habitually angry. I'm not referring to the occasional angry response that is a part of every relationship. I'm referring to when life is characterized by a continual pattern of anger. If a person already has a tendency to be angry, a relationship will bring out this tendency even more. In fact, a relationship can become a sort of factory for the production of anger.

17

If you're in a romantic relationship with a person who is consumed by anger, your love soon wears thin. Anger carelessly expressed will override the love, care, and appreciation that create close relationships because anger erects barriers and leads to aggression.[3]

Red Flag #7: The Attraction Turns Sour

Do you remember the movie *Fatal Attraction?* When I use the term, I'm not referring to a deadly attraction but to an attraction that eventually becomes a repulsion, when what initially drew one person to another later pushes him or her away.

Most of us don't see the potential for this problem at the outset. Fatal attractions occur over a period of time because people naturally show only their best side at the beginning of a relationship. In addition, when people are "falling in love," they tend to see what they want to see and ignore the negatives. I've known individuals who had well-thought-out criteria for what they wanted in a partner but who unfortunately threw that criteria out the window when it came to a certain somebody.

Sometimes an attraction is based on how different the other is. The other person may display characteristics that are extreme or unusual or outside cultural norms. Why are people attracted to such differences? They often make a person stand out as unique, which in turn makes his or her partner feel unique.

What are some of the issues that emerge in fatal attractions? Consider the following case scenarios and ask whether you see yourself in any of these situations.

One woman was attracted to a man who was great fun and a real comic, but she later found out he was too care-free about life. He never took the relationship as seriously as she wanted.

At the beginning of a relationship a man was attracted to how nurturing, loyal, and gentle his girlfriend was, but later he found her to be smothering and codependent.

A woman was at first attracted to how independent a certain man was, but later she thought he was too wrapped up in his own world.

Another lady was drawn to a man of strong character and beliefs, but later she couldn't get past how loud and rude he was.

Do any of these scenarios sound familiar? One client of mine said about his girlfriend, "I like her spunk, but she's too argumentative." Another said he liked his girlfriend's shyness and reserve at first but later saw this as insecurity. These are just some of the many different kinds of fatal attraction.

Avoiding Fatal Attractions

How can you avoid fatal attractions? First of all, don't assume your partner is going to be perfect—confident but humble, spontaneous but organized, pleasant but proactive. Ask yourself, "What do I need for a lifelong commitment?" "What will I not tolerate?" These are important questions to consider before a relationship develops.

Remember that there will always be some differences that bother you. Instead of saying, "This will never work" or "I've got to change my partner" why not ask, "What can I learn from these differences? How might my life be better if I could incorporate some of these differences into my life?"

My wife and I have been married forty-two years. We have similar values and beliefs, and we both have an appreciation for music and education. But we have very different personalities, which determines how you respond to life and do things. On the Myers Briggs Type Indicator test

I'm an ESFJ (Extravert, Sensor, Feeler, Judger). Joyce is an INFP (Introvert, iNtuitive, Feeler, Perceiver). We think, communicate, work, and interact with others very differently. You might say there's a lot of potential for fatal attraction, yet we've been happily married for all these years.

My point is that you have a choice. You can dig in your heels, intensify the way you are, attempt to change the other, and live in misery. Or you can look at the person and say, "I can learn from you. You have something to teach me."

Joyce and I have moved toward one another in our personalities over the years. We accept the uniqueness of one another and have learned to do things "your way." We're still learning. The difference is in the attitude that we choose to have. To learn more about these and other relevant issues, I encourage you to read my book, *Relationships That Work and Those That Don't* (Regal Books, 1998), especially chapters 10 to 14. Here are the chapter titles with descriptions:

Chapter 10—"Compatibility: Dream or Reality?" Becoming compatible is like adapting to life in a foreign land. It can be fun if you don't mind living with a foreigner!

Chapter 11—"How Different Can You Be?" How to spot differences in age, race, culture, and personal habits that could wreck your relationship.

Chapter 12—"If Men Are from Mars and Women from Venus, How on Earth Can They Communicate?" This chapter is about learning to understand and live with the term "opposite," as in "opposite sex."

Chapter 13—"Personality Types: People Who Need People vs. Private Persons." Understanding how personality types differ can enhance your relationship. Accepting the difference is essential!

Chapter 14—"More about Personality Types: Decision Making and Structuring." Whether your relationship is all-out war or purposeful compatibility may depend on these similarities and differences.

Perhaps the best way to tell whether or not differences between you and your partner will lead to a fatal attraction is to perform the following test. In your mind imagine your partner's differences being intensified in the next ten to twenty years. Can you live with these differences? If so, great. If not, it's time to think about ending the relationship.

Red Flag #8: One of You Is a Pursuer

Pursuers relentlessly "chase after" their partners. If the woman of a couple is a pursuer, she doesn't take "no" or "I don't know" for an answer. A man might describe her as a "high-maintenance woman." If she's dating a man and moves too close too soon, he'll push her away, and she'll probably blame him or a defect in herself. When a pursuer is rejected, his or her impulse is to pursue harder.

Some pursuers believe all problems will be solved by "communication," so they fire one question after another and ask to talk about "the relationship." It would be helpful for any pursuer to follow these guidelines from Scripture:

Careless words stab like a sword.
But wise words bring healing.
PROVERBS 12:18 ICB

A person who does not quickly get angry shows that he has understanding.
But a person who quickly loses his temper shows his foolishness.
PROVERBS 14:29 ICB

21

A person who is careful about what he says keeps himself out of trouble.

PROVERBS 21:23 ICB

Sometimes you see people who speak too quickly.
There is more hope for a foolish person than for them.

PROVERBS 29:20 ICB

If a man is a pursuer, he scares women away because he's too much too soon and holds on too tight. He usually gives too many cards, gifts, or compliments. He talks too soon about marriage and children. Sometimes this sort of pursuit borders on overpossessiveness.

Pursuers have a fear of rejection and abandonment. And you've probably already figured out that they create the very thing they fear because of coming on so strong.

Red Flag #9: One of You Is a Distancer

The cry of the distancer is, "Give me freedom and don't fence me in." Most distancers don't make demands and don't want any made of them. To keep from getting close, distancers stop relationships before they start. They look for flaws in the other, and no one will ever meet their standards. Often distancers lash out to hurt their partners before their partners can hurt them. Sometimes the distancer's lack of interest causes his or her partner to come on stronger, and this scares the distancer farther away.

As you think back to your last relationship, did either you or your partner create unreasonable barriers to intimacy? Intimacy is the glue that holds a relationship together, but distancers are afraid of intimacy. They protect themselves against it and use a variety of means to keep others at arm's length.

I talked to someone who dated a distancer for two years and yet was never invited to a family event. Distancers set limits on their time, availability, and on how much they participate in the world of their partners. If you're with a distancer, he or she resists talking about his or her own interests. I've known some distancers who spell out how much they and their partners can spend on gifts, so there are no strings attached.

Red Flag #10: The Man of the Couple Is a "Vanishing Man"

Vanishing men cannot handle the intimacy that is necessary for a healthy relationship. They may come on strong and give you the impression that they are capable of the kind of relationship you want, but then "poof," they vanish. Vanishing men are usually not there when you need them and only want to do what they want to do. If you see this pattern, beware. As soon as possible ask if he has any desire at all to behave differently. If not, believe him and go elsewhere. You're dealing with a man whose relationships are based in fear even though most vanishing men don't like to admit it. He's afraid of intimacy and his feelings are locked away. You may believe you can change him, but remember there are probably six to twelve others before you who used to believe the same.

Intimacy is the glue that holds a relationship together.

One of vanishing man's characteristics is a tendency to feel suffocated in a relationship. He has certain hot buttons that cause him to tune out—like discussions in general, specific emotions, and the topic of commitment.

He may encourage a woman to come close but will also keep her at arm's length. Relationships are not in his comfort zone and when he's uncomfortable, he withdraws.

Here are some more characteristics of a vanishing man:

23

He tries to make you feel guilty or ridiculous for wanting more in a relationship than he's giving.

He wants you to be cheerful regardless of what he does even if he makes no contact with you for weeks.

When he does enter your life again, he expects to pick up right where he left off.

He doesn't do what he says he'll do.

He has little or no empathy for you when you're hurt or upset over his responses.

He is on guard when you probe for his feelings and get into relationship discussions.

Your birthday? Forget it. He does, and may mention it two weeks later.

If you're interested in someone else, he comes on strong, but he expects you to accept his dating others.[4]

We're all called to interact with one another in the way that Colossians 3:12 states: "God has chosen you and made you his holy people. He loves you. So always do these things: Show mercy to others; be kind, humble, gentle, and patient" (icb). If the person you're dating calls this being too pushy, what does it say about his walk with the Lord?

If your partner is a vanishing man, *let him vanish.* A vanishing man does not reflect the qualities of character that we're called to have as believers.

If you think you meet the criteria of a vanishing man, do the following:

1. Look for the fear underlying your pattern.
2. Bring balance into your responses.
3. Begin to do just the opposite of what you've been doing.

4. You may want to talk to a counselor to determine the origins of the way you're responding. If you're still single and really do want a permanent relationship, there is a better way to respond.[5]

Many men and women come into a relationship damaged by neglect, abuse, painful relationship experiences, or lack of role models. Most of us men did not have good male role models in many areas of our lives. Intimacy is scary because most of us were raised to be emotionally handicapped.

In addition, too many today don't understand gender or personality differences, which can add to relationship difficulties. To learn more about these issues, I recommend my book, Communication: Key to Your Marriage. What you read about male-female differences and personality uniqueness could improve your relationships significantly.

If you're a woman looking for a quality man, remember we're all products of our past. Following are some characteristics of a man who is able to grow and change. These have been adapted from a book by Dr. Bonnie Weil. The man who is able to grow and change

is open to learning and once taught begins to put into practice what he has learned

can validate and affirm you

makes his own attempts to reach out and connect with you

is willing for you to nurture him and is learning to nurture you

makes time for you and follows through on time commitments

says he misses you when you've been apart for a while

is willing to learn to engage on an emotional level

Remember there are some men who are like a butterfly. If you chase them, you'll never catch them, but if you stand still, one might come and sit next to you.[6]

Red Flag #11: One of You Has a Habit of Saying, "I Love You, But . . ."

Watch out for Mr. or Miss "I love you, but . . ." When you become involved with someone who spouts this line, get out! Run! It's an exercise in futility. This is the phrase of those who have what some call "commitment ambivalence."

Some people cannot bring themselves to say those important three words, "I love you." Some fake it by mumbling or making a joke of it. Others use substitute phrases such as, "Now I *really* do like you a lot," or "I really care for you," or "I think the world of you." What's really painful is when early on a partner can't stop telling you, "I love you," which makes you feel wanted, desirable, and special, but then a new phrase crops up: "I love you, but . . ." Have you ever heard any of the following examples?

"I love you, but I need more time."

"I love you, but I can't live with you."

"I love you, but we're too different."

"I love you, but you're too good for me."

"I love you, but I love Andrew more."

"I love you, but it would never work out."

"I love you, but I have to marry someone else."

"I love you, but I need to work things out."

"I love you, but I need to be alone."

"I love you, but my career isn't far enough along."

And let's not forget the classic, "I love you, but I'm not *in love* with you."[7] What's even worse is when a person says, "I love you" out loud but reserves the last phrase ("but...") for an internal conversation with him- or herself.

A counselee named Theresa said, "It was strange. I guess I had selective hearing. He told me again and again, 'I love you, but...,' yet I heard only the first three words."

When Is It Time to Break Up?

A client in her late twenties shared with me, "It's so hard because I don't hate him. He really is a nice person, but he's just not for me. It would be so much easier if he were a rat and I could despise him, but I don't!"

You don't have to hate or even dislike a person for it to be necessary to break up. If the relationship isn't beneficial for you, it's not for the other person either, regardless of what he or she says.

I've also heard people say, "If the relationship was meant to be over, I wouldn't doubt my decision, would I? I seem to waver back and forth." But the truth is wavering back and forth is normal. Even if you give your partner a list of eight things to change and he or she does all eight, it's being done *for you*. Unless he or she wants to change because he or she sees the value in doing so, the changes are not likely to last.

Your relationship needs to be cut off when (a) you want out more than you want in, or (b) both of you want out and neither of you wants to work on continuing the relationship. Sometimes a couple will say, "We'll still see each other as 'friends' because we enjoy each other's company." My question is why. This keeps you from investing time and energy in recovering and then finding someone who could be your lifelong companion.

When is it best to break off a relationship? *As soon as you know it's not going to work out.* You need to listen to your heart, your thoughts, and the Lord's guidance. Trust yourself. Parts of the relationship may be positive, but are these strong enough to carry the rest of it? Once you know it's not going to work out, the time you spend waiting is wasted because it delays your recovery and thus the development of a new relationship. Watch out for immobilizing statements that will keep you trapped. They include:

"I just hate hurting another person."

"What will everyone think?"

"What if he gets really angry with me? I can't handle that."

"I don't know what to say or how to do it."

"It's just too difficult."

Every time you make such a statement, you begin to believe it even more, and it becomes more difficult to do what needs to be done.

Breaking Off an Engagement

Perhaps one of the most difficult relationships to break off is an engagement. But as painful as a broken engagement is, it is nowhere near as devastating as a divorce can be. Over the years I've heard many people say, "I knew in the first year that I'd made a mistake," or "It was the second week of the honeymoon that I knew I should have listened to those warning signals inside my head." Perhaps the most drastic one came from a young man who was divorcing his wife. He said he knew as soon as he married her that he had made a mistake. And when I asked him how soon he was aware of this, he said he realized it as she was walking down the aisle. How tragic!

Unfortunately, many people still believe that an engagement has the same level of commitment as a marriage. It doesn't. Approximately 40 to 50 percent of engagements in our country break up. Over the past five years, of all the couples that I have seen in premarital counseling, 25 to 30 percent decided not to marry and some at the last minute. In all but two of these cases, the couple made the decision themselves without my having to recommend this step. A friend of mine shared with me that 80 percent of the couples he works with in premarital counseling make a decision not to marry. Over the years I've seen couples who have canceled the wedding just a week or two prior to the wedding date.

One woman in her twenties realized that she didn't fully love the quality young man to whom she was engaged. She had hoped that after being married she would fall in love with him. Two weeks prior to the wedding, which would have been a very large and elaborate service and reception, she told her father, "Dad, I have some bad news for you. I'm sorry because it's going to cost you a lot of money for nothing, but I just don't love my fiancé. It would be wrong to go through with this wedding." Her father responded, "Honey, don't be concerned about the money. I'm more concerned about you and your happiness. Whatever you feel is best, I'll back you." And the wedding was canceled. Two years later she met the man who was to become her husband. Her act took courage. It was disappointing and painful to many people, but some of the wisest decisions of life are.

Here's some good advice to keep in mind from a rabbi who wrote the book, *Dating Secrets of the Ten Commandments:*

29

How do you feel when you know a relationship is "right"? When it makes you feel alive and optimistic for your future together. When it heightens your sensitivity and enjoyment of even the most common experience.

If you no longer look forward to seeing her, if you no longer laugh at his jokes, if she irritates you, if he bores you, then you are in trouble. If you secretly fantasize about her being abducted by space aliens while crossing the road, or hear yourself suggesting to him that he volunteer as a freedom fighter in Bosnia, it is time to end the relationship.

Do not make the mistake of staying with an unsatisfactory relationship out of a sense of guilt. Many women I know are prone to staying with a mean and angry man whom they are "not sure about" even after a lot of time together. Forget about it! "But I love him" is no reason to stay with a louse.

You know when you are in love, and when this ain't it, dump the schlump. Don't stay in an unhappy relationship because you are afraid of hurting his feelings, or, worse, because you fear nothing better will come along. And stop trying to be the Messiah with every guy. Some men are beyond redemption. You are entitled to happiness, so drop the suffering servant posture. If you deny your essential need to feel loved and appreciated for too long, you will either die on the inside or explode on the outside. That is unfair to both of you. By being honest and ending the relationship you will free yourself and your partner to go out and find new dates who are more suitable. You will both be happier.[8]

Red Herrings
Reasons People Fail to End a Relationship

Letting go of someone can be difficult, no matter how unhealthy the relationship may be. We get attached to people with whom we've spent a lot of time, so when speaking of a breakup, the phrase "letting go" is a little misleading. A more accurate phrase would be "ripping apart," which communicates the pain involved in separation. But if a relationship needs to be terminated, prolonging the breakup will only intensify the eventual pain. In this chapter we'll look at some distractions that keep people from ending unhealthy relationships. I call these distractions "red herrings."

Red Herring #1: A Partner's Feelings

Often people get wrapped up in the other person's feelings. Most of us don't want to cause another person pain.

Even if breaking up is the healthiest decision for both parties, someone is going to get hurt, if not both people. Also, if a partner tends to be an obsessive lover, it will be difficult to break free of him or her. He or she will hang on like superglue and pursue you in countless ways.

A thirty-year-old woman described the roller-coaster ride she felt she was on while she struggled through the termination of a relationship: "I thought I was going crazy. My feelings were in turmoil. One minute I seemed to delight in Troy, but then I felt controlled and oppressed by him. One minute I loved him, but the next I resented him and what he did. Oh, he was attentive, that's for sure, but he didn't know when to stop. I felt invaded by him. And now, when I try to break it off, I feel guilty. What's wrong with me?"

It sounds like she wanted in and out of the relationship at the same time. Many women hang onto unhealthy relationships. They're hoping that somehow the man will magically turn into Prince Charming. But as one radio personality said, "When you kiss a toad and he doesn't turn into a prince—you just get slime in your mouth."

Of course, one way to counteract such thinking is to realize the longer you put off the inevitable, the more you shortchange yourself. You are hurting yourself as much if not more than the other person.

Red Herring #2: Sexual Pleasure

Another reason people fail to break up is because of the power of sexual pleasure. Though Scripture and many psychological and sociological studies speak with one voice about the destructive consequences of premarital sex, the fact is many people engage in it. If a member of a couple who has been sexually intimate knows it would be best to sever the relationship, oftentimes memories of intense pleasure prevent him or her from doing so. He or she begins to listen to hormones instead of reason.

If your partner is seductive and discovers he or she can use sexual activity to keep you on the leash, you will be controlled in more ways than you realize. Also, if sex is part of your relationship, you might stay with a person who is sexually safe rather than run the risk of getting involved with a person with an STD.

When couples who are sleeping together or cohabiting come to me for premarital counseling, I ask them to stop sleeping together for several reasons. One reason is to determine what's holding their relationship together—physical gratification or something else. Some such couples who thought they would be together forever break up soon after the sex is gone. They discover they really didn't care for each other as people.

> *Sex in a premarital relationship is a roadblock to genuine intimacy.*

Sex in a premarital relationship is a roadblock to genuine intimacy. When sex is involved before a foundation of love has been built, more likely than not it limits the couple's chances of building a relationship with which both members of the couple will be happy.

Red Herring #3: Excuses

You may begin to make excuses for the other person or the relationship:

"It's not as bad as it seems."

"He or she will change. I'm just impatient."

"I've invested four years. What's another year? It could work out."

"They're just slower in the commitment process than I am."

"He's not the best catch, but neither am I. How do I know I'll find anyone better?"

Just remember that excuses are just that—excuses. They only delay the inevitable, and the longer you use them, the more pain you'll cause to both you and your partner.

Red Herring #4: A Need for Security

You may stay in a poor relationship because you're addicted to security. As bad as a relationship might be, people feel safer staying in a relationship about which they know something than venturing out into the unknown. Sometimes you can be addicted to a person even when you want him or her out of your life. An individual's need to have someone in his or her life sometimes overrides that individual's ability to wait for the right someone. There is such a need that anyone will do.

Red Herring #5: Settling for "Making Do"

A client named Phil shared another reason many people hesitate to break up: "I know what I want in a relationship. I thought it through carefully and I have my list, but I'm just not sure I'll be able to find what I want. I've got to compromise, I guess, but it is very uncomfortable. Some days I feel it's best to get out and then I think, 'I'll never find her anyway,' so I just make do." The fact is making do doesn't last a lifetime. If all you can hope for in a relationship is to "make do," you're doing a disservice to you and your partner to continue the relationship.

Red Herring #6: "I Love Him"

Many people stay in a relationship because they think they're in love. The kind of love they are experiencing, however, is coming from defeats from the past or because of mistaking a sexual involvement for love.

Some people live their lives on the phrase, "But I love him . . ." or "But I love her . . ." Basing a decision for life on fickle, misleading feelings is a good way to keep yourself in pain. I've heard both men and women say, "I just love that person. Oh, I know they're . . . , but . . ." The words I've heard people use to describe their partners range anywhere from cold, angry, and controlling to uncommunicative, distant, abusive, and violent. Remember, the words "I love him" don't erase your partner's shortcomings.[1]

Red Herring #7: Comments from Friends and Family

Friends and family can have enormous influence, either for good or for bad. Jim Smoke in his ministry to the divorced describes the dilemma this way:

> You may be getting pressure from your family and friends. They keep saying, "Come on. How long is it going to take? You know you're right for one another. You've just got the typical jitters that anyone has. Go on, tie the knot." And you begin to think, "Well, if they think we're right for each other, maybe there's something that I'm missing." But pressure like this you don't need. You must be certain. Letting someone else make a decision for you won't work since they don't have to live with the decision, you do.[2]

Watch out for comments from friends and especially relatives. You might hear some of the following:

"I can't believe it. You've wasted so much time!"

"Oh . . . are you sure? You don't want to make a hasty decision and regret it later."

"I thought he was just perfect for you."

"I'll really miss him. He was becoming just like one of the family."

"Are you sure? You're not getting any younger."

"Did you pray about this and ask for God's will in this decision?"

"Did you discuss this with your pastor?"

"I hope you didn't go too far. You could end up with a disease and then everyone else will know what you were doing."

"I always knew you could do better. I tried to warn you, but you had to learn for yourself. Look at how much time you wasted."

Years ago I was doing premarital counseling with a couple who had been going together for five years, but it wasn't working out because of numerous differences and problems. I finally suggested that they put the relationship and pending marriage on hold to work on their own individual issues. The response I heard was, "Finally someone has given us permission *not* to marry. We've been getting all this pressure from our families to 'tie the knot.'" The sigh of relief I heard from them is a sigh that many experience when they make this decision. Don't let your family run your life.

Red Herring #8: Mind Games and Promises

There are certain "mind games" that can keep people from breaking off a going-nowhere relationship. People begin to think, "Perhaps all we need is some time apart from one another and then we'll see things clearer. A trial separation would really help us." All this does is postpone the inevitable and prolong the recovery.

Your memory may be selective and emphasize the good times or positives. And if your partner knows how to activate these memories, he or she may try to get you to hesitate, waver, and postpone what needs to be done.

Watch out for promises from your ex-partner. If his or her promises to change were sincere, they could have been made earlier. Now such promises are more than likely a desperate attempt to prevent you from going forward with your plans.

Red Herring #9: Emotional Rescue

Emotional rescue is when one person tries to rescue another person from some sort of pain, whether it be from a death in the family, a divorce, or whatever. In relationships like these, it's very common for the rescuer to begin to feel overwhelmed by the other's incessant need for attention.

Habitual rescuers always feel a need to be in a relationship, regardless of whether the other person is a good match. Sometimes emotional rescue goes both ways—both partners are trying to fill an emotional gap in the other. Many such couples live together because each person has a need to be with someone, to be beside another body. Often the couple knows the relationship is not going anywhere, but the members of the couple do not break up because they feel safe with what's familiar. An individual in this kind of relationship often won't end it until he or she sees a different relationship possibility. In this way such people avoid the loneliness that is a regular part of being single after a relationship ends.

Making the Best Decision

If you're in a relationship that's on a fast track to nowhere, but you're stuck, can you identify what's holding you back? It may help to conduct an REA—Relationship Evaluation Analysis. Just as we do in marriage counseling, let's begin with the positives. List ten positive qualities of the other person that you really appreciate.

1.
2.
3.
4.
5.
6.
7.
8.
9.
10.

Neil Clark Warren has said that most individuals have must-have and can't-stand lists. Do the above qualities match up with your "must-have" characteristics? Some of the "must-haves" that many singles have identified are emotional health, strong character, financial security, verbal intimacy, shared interests, similar values, and ambition.[3]

Now list ten qualities or characteristics of the other person that bother you.

1.
2.
3.
4.
5.
6.
7.

8.
9.
10.

Dr. Warren has a list of twenty-five "Can't Stands" that singles have identified. Do you have such a list? Have you ever listed them? These are characteristics of another person to which you respond so negatively that you wouldn't choose to spend the rest of your life with that person. Some of the items on Dr. Warren's list were lying, cheating, dominating, financial irresponsibility, anger mismanagement, pornography, and procrastination.[4] Does your list of ten negative qualities bear a resemblance to your can't-stand list?

Now that you've thought through the qualities of the other person, let's go a step further. What are six reasons why this relationship is not the best for you?

1.
2.
3.
4.
5.
6.

What is the message of this list? Usually it's "Leave!"

If you're ambivalent about ending your relationship, yet you know you should, perhaps it would help to make a list of eight to ten consequences of staying with your partner. Perhaps seeing the consequences on paper will jar you into action. Here are some other questions to consider:

1. What is your partner not being or doing that you want?
2. How long have you been thinking about ending the relationship?

3. What would have to happen for you to feel this might work out?
4. How often have you brought up your concerns to your partner? What has happened since then?
5. Are you in a situation in which your partner is willing to do anything, but that doesn't matter to you anymore?
6. What emotional effect does your partner have on you?
7. Does your partner's attitude and behavior toward you increase your positive feelings about yourself?
8. Do you feel more attractive being with him or her?
9. Does your partner bring out the best or worst in you?
10. Is your partner trustworthy?
11. Do you constantly make excuses for him or her? Do you and your partner constantly try to change one another?
12. Is your relationship with Jesus Christ enhanced by being with him or her?

I hope this chapter has helped you discern whether it's necessary for you to break up with your partner. Ending a relationship is difficult to do, but if it's necessary, the painful reality is the sooner you break up, the better. The most loving thing you can do for your partner and for yourself is end the relationship.

Calling It Quits
How to End a Relationship

The Stages of Ending a Relationship

Usually the process of a breakup involves five stages:

1. awareness
2. doubt and confusion
3. marking time
4. testing the waters
5. breakup

In the "awareness" stage one or both members of the couple begin to wonder about the future of the relationship because the infatuation phase is now past. Problems, conflicts, and major differences that were initially dismissed or denied now seem more prominent.

The next stage, "doubt and confusion," is when one member of the couple is unsure about his or her feelings for the other. There's some disinterest, but he or she is uncertain whether it's a fleeting experience or something that's going to remain.

Then you move into the "marking time" stage. This is when the attraction begins to dwindle in earnest, so a positive future is dim. The relationship is at a standstill, and the only reason a breakup has not occurred yet is because the partner who knows he or she will have to break up eventually is sad about the prospect. He or she is aware of how much pain the breakup will cause both parties.

The fourth stage, "testing the waters," is when the person who is about to break up begins to move away from the relationship, subtly but consistently. She makes excuses when she misses a date, politely asks for more space, and spends more time with her friends. She begins to think about how to let the other person know and wonders what her future will be like without the other.

The "breakup" comes when the initiator realizes this cannot be delayed any longer. He or she will have more anxiety about not breaking up than with the breakup itself.[1]

Breakup Styles

How do you break up? What do you say? Many people who know they need to end their relationships don't want to be seen as the "bad guy," so they behave in such a way that prompts the other person to make the decision and take the necessary steps. The best advice I can give you about this breakup style is *don't do it*. It's irresponsible and usually ineffective.

Another bad approach is the Bermuda Triangle Technique. You've probably heard stories about ships that enter this part of the Atlantic Ocean never to be heard from again. There's no explanation for what happens to these ships; they simply disappear. Unfortunately, some people break up by disappearing. They change jobs, move out of the state, or disconnect their phones to terminate a relationship. Again, this is an irresponsible, heartless, and just plain wrong way to end a relationship.

Don't be overly concerned with hurting your partner, or you'll never do what needs to be done.

To break up in a mature, responsible way will take courage on your part, and you can count on feeling uncomfortable. Breaking up is rarely easy, though a feeling of relief usually follows. Don't be overly concerned with hurting your partner, or you'll never do what needs to be done. Be honest and simply accept that your partner is going to be upset and maybe even angry. He or she may retaliate by telling lies about you and could contaminate some of your mutual friendships. All of this is par for the course and shouldn't deter you.

If you're in a relationship but want out, why do you want out? What are your reasons? Take the time to write them out clearly, so you don't have second thoughts.

The authors of *He's Scared, She's Scared* offer some helpful suggestions for people considering a breakup:

Don't become aloof, critical or irritable. Don't try to engage your partner into a quarrel. Don't make hints or leave evidence around that you are interested in someone else. If you're going out on a special occasion, be on your best behavior. Don't create a miserable situation. Don't become irritable or angry if your partner becomes nicer, more loving or more cooperative as they try to hang on to you.

Don't use the typical leaving excuses such as: "I think we need to see less of one another" or "Perhaps we both need to date others for a while" or "You need to move on with your life and I'll just hold you back."

Some like to use the fade out approach. You've seen this on videos where the scene gradually fades out into nothing. Some are so slight you don't realize that it's happening until the misty scene fades into nothing. If you fade away, it will be noticed. Don't break up in steps. If you're going to break up, do it carefully, sensibly and completely.

It may help to take some time and write out your reasons. Rehearse what you want to say. Explain yourself carefully.

Some are able to share the ending face to face with their partner.

Some give them a letter of explanation and have them read it while they are there.

Some conduct the breakup over the phone while others do it with a letter.[2]

Here are some facts to keep in mind about breaking off a relationship. Both parties will have a tendency to blame, but breakups are no one's fault. When you enter into a relationship, breaking up is one of the natural outcomes. Part of the purpose of entering into a relationship is to discover whether the person you're with is the person you want to be with for the rest of your life. You can choose to see your relationship as a waste of time or a mistake, or you can choose to view it as a time when you investigated the possibility of a lifelong partner and your decision was no.

No matter how careful you are, how delicately honest and sensitive, your partner may not understand. In fact, expect to be misunderstood and disliked, and you'll be better prepared.

Be aware that you may be tempted to lie about your reasons for breaking up to reduce the pain of the other or to get out of the relationship more quickly than you would by telling the truth. This is a normal temptation, but don't succumb to it. Tell the truth.

Second thoughts are normal too. You may be convinced this is the right move after thoroughly evaluating the situation, but second thoughts still come: "Perhaps it would have worked" or "Maybe I'm overreacting" or "Another week wouldn't hurt."[3] It's good to be aware of these second thoughts, but it is unwise to trust them.

What should you say? The classic line is plain, straightforward, and to the point: "I do care about you, but now it's really more of a friendship. You've got a lot of wonderful qualities and our relationship hasn't been bad, but something is missing."

A friend of mine put together a list of statements that Christian women often use to break up:

1. "I've found someone more spiritual."
2. "It's not God's will."
3. "I feel called to mission work very far away from you as soon as possible."
4. "It could never work—I'm sanguine and you're phlegmatic."
5. "God loves me and *must* have a better plan for my life."
6. "I feel like I'm dating my brother."
7. "At least I got a lot out of our Bible studies together."
8. "You need someone with lower standards."
9. "I think we should just be prayer partners."
10. "I do love you, but it's just agape love now."

How would you feel if someone used one of these lines on you? Not very good, I suspect, so it would be a good idea to refrain from using them on your partner.

The "simultaneous" approach is when two mature adults come to a mutual decision that the relationship isn't going anywhere and probably won't in the future. They show concern for each other and part ways peaceably.[4] It would be nice if all breakups were like this, but they're usually much more difficult.

The Right Way to Break Up

Consider these suggestions. Decide whether you want to do this in person, over the phone, or in a letter. And whatever you do, if you are serious about not seeing this person again, don't be vague or give double messages or leave the door open.

If your decision comes during a first date or you keep running into the person at work, talking face-to-face is probably a good idea. If you've been in a long-term relationship, sometimes writing a letter is the better way to go because the person can't respond immediately, has to think about it, and can't pressure you to change your mind. Your partner will want and need to talk to you at some time, however. Whatever you do, don't let your partner hear it from someone else.

Be gracious and polite. You could share something positive at the same time you let them know you would prefer not going out with them again. Statements like, "Thank you, but I would rather not," work well. However, if you add the phrase "right now" or "at this time," your partner is likely to think your resistance is temporary and you'll be back. Don't say "I'll get back to you" or "Call me later" unless you want the relationship to continue.

Make it genuine. You may want to say, "Thank you for the time you've invested, but I'm not interested in pursuing the relationship any further." You don't have to give them a list of your reasons if you don't want to. If he or she presses you for more information, you have the option of simply repeating your initial statement word for word. Sometimes all reasons do is give the other person an opportunity to call your decision into question, which is bad for everyone concerned.

However, if it's possible to have an open discussion without a lot of mudslinging and defensiveness, talking about your reasons for breaking up can be an opportunity for personal growth for both you and your ex-partner. If you decide to do this, be sure to explain to your partner that your reasons are just that—your reasons. They are the problems as you see them, and you don't expect the other person to agree with you in every case. Keep in mind that no matter how the other person responds, he or she is responsible for it. Don't take responsibility for the actions and words of another.

If there are any items for you to return, it's best to do so at this time. If things need to be moved, do this as soon as possible.

If your partner has been deceitful, lied about who he or she is, was less than trustworthy about his or her work or financial status, told fibs about his or her Christian beliefs, harassed you sexually, stole from you, or was unfaithful to you, you should confront him or her. I've seen too many situations in which the person was let off the hook with no confrontation. The individual was never exposed for what he or she is, and such people desperately need to experience the natural consequences and discomfort of their sinful behavior. They need to experience conviction and come to genuine repentance, so others don't fall prey to their pattern of destructive behaviors. Remember, if your partner did it to you, he or she will do it to others.

I've seen cases in singles fellowship groups when a person has been asked to leave the group because of a pattern of non-Christian behavior such as stealing or date rape. And it doesn't take long for the word to get out.

If you think it's time to end a relationship, don't drop hints or expect your partner to know what you're thinking and feeling. Hints are missed, avoided, or misinterpreted, and people generally are not very good at mind reading. Avoid breaking dates, "forgetting" them, or changing plans over and over.

If your partner senses that you're pulling away or resistant to moving on, but you haven't made your intentions clear, here's what to expect. Imagine two people walking along side by side and hand in hand. Now imagine that one of them begins to slow down and fall behind. His or her partner hangs on tighter and tries to pull the slower one forward. In the same way, you can expect your partner to start pulling you to him or her, which probably won't be a pleasant experience for either of you. This is one of many reasons why being clear about your intentions is important.

Plan in advance what you think you will need to say and practice making these statements aloud if you know this will be difficult for you. You should not be subtle or appear uncertain, especially if the other person doesn't want to hear what you're saying or is resistant to the whole idea. Don't let the other person back you into a corner or get you in a defensive position. You could use statements like the following:

"I understand this is upsetting, but our times together are over. This is not something I want to discuss because it's nonnegotiable."

"I'm going to hang up now. It won't help either of us to continue to talk, and if you call again, I will hang up."

"Please don't contact me in any way. It's better that we go our separate ways."

"What you're doing feels like harassment, and if you continue, I will obtain a restraining order so we can both go on with our lives."

Unfortunately, some people do not know how to take no for an answer. Your partner may be obsessed with you, addicted to having a relationship, or so hurt and angry that he or she wants to make life miserable for you. If so, it's important to be (a) assertive and (b) proactive about your safety. If for any reason you're scared to break up because you think you would be in physical danger, ask your pastor or a couple of close friends to be present with you when you break the news to your partner. If you ever feel like you're in danger, remember that you can almost always pick up a phone and call 911.

Unfortunately, some people do not know how to take no for an answer.

Sometimes the reluctant partner believes he or she knows your thoughts and feelings better than you do, so whatever you say may not register. The more information you give, the more you build the other's hope that you are not serious. The more you explain, the more you encourage them to persist. Clients have told me, "It seems cruel to be this way" or "It feels mean to break up like this." While I can appreciate the compassion from which these statements come, they are simply not true. Breaking up is not easy, it's hard, but it's also necessary, for you and your partner. What is cruel is hanging on and prolonging a relationship that's going nowhere when you know it's over.

You may need to take some further steps to get the message through such as screening all calls with an answering machine, changing your phone listing to an unlisted number, telling mutual friends to alert you if your former partner is coming to an activity, or suggesting to your friends that you would rather not be invited to events to which he or she is coming.[5]

Dealing with Other People

It's important to be proactive in your relationships with other people too. One of the best ways I've seen people inform their friends and family about a breakup is by sending a letter that states what happened, how it has impacted you, and the best way for them to respond to you. People do this all the time for other traumatic events —deaths in the family, divorces, contractions of a fatal disease—so why shouldn't you do the same for the trauma involved in a breakup?

In your letter don't apologize to yourself or anyone else. If this was a necessary step, it's positive (although painful) and should be expressed in a positive way. Here's a brief example of what one friend wrote to another: "I just wanted to let you know where I am in my life right now. I've made a painful but positive step. I've broken off my relationship of ____ months with _____. I feel this is best for all concerned, and it will take me some time to readjust my life. I appreciate your support and accepting this brief version of what's occurred."

This is honest, brief, and lets the friend know in a kind way not to press for details. You're not under any obligation to give more details than you want to give. You don't need to convince others of the validity of your decision. If someone doesn't understand, you don't have to help him or her understand. In fact, some people won't understand no matter how much you try to explain it. If someone persists in wanting to know more, either repeat what you said word for word or use and repeat the following phrase as many times as you need to: "Thank you for understanding and not pushing me for details at this time."

Here's another version of a short letter: "After careful consideration and thoughtful discussions about our relationship, _____ and I have decided to stop seeing one another. This will give each of us the opportunity to go on with our lives in a new way. I'm sure it will take some time for each of us to adjust before considering future relationships." This last sentence is important because it tells others not to try setting you up with others right away.

You could write a form letter for all your family and friends. It might look something like this:

Dear Family and Friends,

Because you are significant to me, I wanted to share with you a recent event in my life that will probably affect me for some time. As you know, _____ and I have been dating exclusively for three years. It appeared to us and to many others that we were on our way to marriage, but this is no longer the case. I have decided it would be best for us to dissolve our relationship. I'm sorry for the disappointment this may cause you as well as any feelings of awkwardness you experience, because many of you are friends of both _____ and me. For some of you, this will mean a loss of doing things with us as a couple as we have done in the past. So it will take some adjustment on your part as well as ours.

You may be wondering how to respond to me and what to talk about and what not to say. Actually, you can feel free to respond to me as you have in the past. I can handle references about _____ and me. It's not something you have to avoid. I doubt, however, that I'll go into any more detail about this decision, but you can rest assured that this is the best thing for me. Thank you for your support and your prayers.

Sincerely, _____

If the breakup was traumatic, it might be helpful to tell people that the breakup was devastating and that you will cry and be upset from time to time. Let them know specifically what you need from them. Also, let them know that you may be recovering for several months; this is to help people have a realistic timetable for your recovery. You're likely to go into greater detail with close friends and relatives, of course, but this letter will protect you from having to share the situation over and over again, which can be exhausting and painful.

On the Receiving End

What if you're the one being let go? Let's say you've been given some clear or even unclear indications that your partner is not as interested now as he or she used to be. It's important to avoid holding on to your partner. Avoid trying to prove to your partner that he or she doesn't know a good thing when he or she has it. You can't prove to another that you're the best one for him or her. Your partner needs to discover this alone, otherwise you'll end up on a performance treadmill. If you're in a relationship in which you have to prove to your partner that you're the right one, you're not in the right relationship.

If you sense he or she wants to go, one of the best things you can do is offer to let him or her go. You might say, "Listen, I sense that you're wanting to end our relationship. While I like you and would like to continue our relationship, I realize how silly it is to hold on to you if you don't want to be held. I'd like to let you go." If you choose to say something like this, you have to be entirely ready to make good on your offer—to walk away from that person forever—but if you can do it, in the end you'll save yourself a lot of pain.

I've seen so many people mistreated by the person who is breaking up. Generally, people on the receiving end tolerate way too much. Instead of confronting and discussing what is taking place in the relationship, some actually become more accepting, even when they are not being treated well. Don't be a doormat! All this does is reinforce negative behavior on the part of the other person.

Here's another approach, a better one: document what you see occurring. You might tell your partner, "On this date you told me such and such. And then on this date you did or said . . . This confuses me and perhaps you're a bit confused as well. Perhaps you need to take some time to figure out your feelings. When you have done so, let's talk about it. I'll wait to hear from you. And if I don't, that too is an answer."

Don't be that accommodating and accessible. If your partner calls you after being out of contact for a while, don't drop everything to match his schedule. Work him into your own schedule. And if you hear excuses about his "come close, go away" behavior or if he tells you he would change if you were different, don't buy it. Say, "No, I didn't ask you for excuses or complaints. Those I'm not interested in. It appears you're pulling away. Just tell me what you want. Do you want a relationship or not?" Blunt? Yes! Is it possible you'll get a painful answer? Yes! But even if you do, you'll have an opportunity to recover and go on with your life, rather than wallowing in years of your partner's indecision.

Here are some good rules of thumb if you find yourself on the receiving end of a breakup:

Avoid the phone trap—waiting by it or using it to check up on your partner.

Establish a gag rule on what you talk about with others. If you need to talk about your relationship, limit it to a five-minute summary.

Keep busy and involved with others. The "sit around and wait" routine is counterproductive.

53

I remember one of my female clients saying, "I feel like I'm on an emotional roller coaster. One day he's kind, consistent, and follows through. Then there's no call when he said he'd call. I've changed my plans to accommodate his plans and then he changes plans without warning. That puts me in a panic since I've got to make sure my two children are taken care of, and you can't always make those changes with babysitters."

Henry Cloud and John Townsend said:

In relationships, you get what you tolerate. Why we are not sure. In part it is because people who allow people to get away with things seem to attract the kind that would want to get away with less-than-considerate behavior. Another reason seems to be that whenever we do not have good limits with each other, there is a regression on the part of the person who is enabled to be less than mature.

In any case, you can bet that for the most part, especially in the world of dating, *you will get what you tolerate.*

Set your limits and stick to them. Tell the person that you won't tolerate certain things and if they continue, he or she cannot see you until they learn how to not act that way. This is another advantage of doing this early. You don't yet have a lot to lose.

Remember, we are not talking about sending the person away after one small offense. If you are like that, he or she would do well to have some limits set with you! Remember, it is a glory to not make an issue out of everything. But, if it is significant, and if it is a pattern, then deal with it early. You will be glad you did.[6]

When a partner is backing away from you, the best thing you can do is back away yourself. But explain your reasons for doing this. Let him or her know that his or her behavior is unacceptable. He or she is either in the relationship or out of it. Let your partner know that you'll not tolerate any cat-and-mouse middle ground.

Part 2

Getting Over the Loss of a Relationship

Breakup Blues

"Let's just be friends." Have you ever heard those fateful words? Or how about, "I think it would be better if we stopped seeing each other"? Heartbreak, disappointment, loneliness, numbness—these are our feelings when we experience a broken relationship.

One of the greatest delights in life is loving another person, but one of the greatest disappointments in life is being in love with a person who neither loves you nor wants to be a part of your life any longer. In addition, every survivor of a broken relationship is haunted by the residue of fear about future relationships. The trauma of a lost love is one of life's most painful hurts, and anxiety about loving again is one of life's greatest fears.

The Impact Phase

The initial response is often a sense of unreality. "This must be happening to someone else. It couldn't be happening to me." Some have said they felt like they were frozen in time. Everything just stood still. Others have said they actually pinched themselves because it was like a bad dream or a nightmare; they just wanted to wake up and discover it wasn't real.

If the loss was intense, you'll feel numb for a couple of days and then the intensity of all the emotions will hit. For some, the devastation and intensity of emotions isn't much different than that of experiencing the death of a close friend or family member.

Sometimes the first few days after a breakup occurs is referred to as the *Impact Phase*. When two cars hit each other, it's called an impact. And you know the result of that—damage. The pain you experience will depend on the length and intensity of the relationship and on your reluctance to have it end.

A female client of mine in her early thirties said, "It feels as though I was driving along a nice residential street in a new car and all of a sudden someone backed out of a driveway and just blindsided me. Not only that, they didn't stop to see what damage they did. They just hit me and drove off. So I'm left to deal with the damage all by myself. I feel victimized."

If your ex-partner has just broken up with you, you probably long for the relationship you once had. For some, this longing becomes an obsession dominating every waking moment. Nothing has meaning until the relationship is restored, but restoration of the relationship exactly as it was happens very infrequently.

What's your initial week going to be like? You could experience any or all of the following:

You may have difficulty concentrating. Your mind returns to the relationship and you replay the events again and again.

You may watch the phone and your computer waiting for a call or an e-mail.

You may listen to sad songs and personalize them.

You may either spend time making plans for how to get the person back or focus on why it's best you're not in the relationship anymore.

You may rehearse events and conversations to determine what went wrong and what you could have done or said differently.

You may recall the good times and wonder if any of the positive statements your ex-partner made were true.

You may focus on what you could do differently, such as dressing more stylishly or being more sensitive to draw him or her back. You may concentrate on only the positive experiences and blank out the bad times.

Guilt is likely to be your constant companion whether it's warranted or not.

You may think of ways to get even or make your ex-partner feel the pain.

In heartbreak, it's not just a heart that is shattered but a dream as well. It feels as though your life has been stopped cold. You're sitting there holding the pieces of your heart in your hands, and time is moving forward while leaving you in its wake. And the more life moves on, the more you feel you can never catch up. You're in a state of painful suspended animation.[1]

"I wish I could quit thinking about her," one of my young male clients told me. "We went together for three years.

I just assumed we'd get married. What I got instead was dumped. I never knew I could feel this bad. I feel like I'm going through a divorce, but at least divorced people have recovery groups to help them. There's nothing for me. I wake up and there she is—sitting in my thought life, taking over the day. I wish there was an antimemory pill." Unfortunately, there's no such pill. You remember the good times as well as the hurts and the mistakes, and each memory activates pain.

You remember the good times as well as the hurts and the mistakes, and each memory activates pain.

The pain is intensified by the feeling that no one else really understands. The grief you feel in this loss can be as intense as a loss by death, but you don't have the support of others as you do when someone dies. No one sends a card or brings over a casserole. You're wounded by the comments and lack of understanding of others. Some chide you with "I told you so" or "You should have seen the problem coming." Others push you, saying, "Get on with your life" or "There are plenty of others out there and better than what you had." All these comments hurt. They don't help.

If depression is now part of your life, expect its symptoms to be with you for a while. Difficulties with sleeping, eating, lack of interest, lethargy, neglect, tears, anger, a negative outlook on life—these are normal responses.

Whether a person has lost someone in death, divorce, or a breakup, sometimes it's helpful to think of all the pain and trauma as one big "ball of grief." This is helpful for two reasons: it helps you put a label on what you are experiencing and it also normalizes what you're feeling. It's not wrong to experience this jumbled pile of emotions, it's normal. What you're going through is no different than what others experience when going through a similar set of circumstances.

Some of the men and women who hurt the most are those who are still deeply attached to former spouses or fiancés and want their relationships to be restored. They feel desperate, totally out of control, and willing to do almost anything to keep their partners. But they have no control over the decisions of those they love. Being out of control in any situation is fearful, but having no control over a broken relationship is worse. Watching your loved one slip away without any recourse leaves you feeling empty and impotent. You feel as if you're unraveling emotionally.

Why Does It Hurt So Much?

Why do these broken relationships hit us so hard? Part of the happiness in a close, loving relationship comes from being loved by the other person. Consider the parent-child relationship. Usually it is a two-way love relationship. If your father (or mother) dies, you know he didn't die because he stopped caring for you. He simply died, and you accept that. When a pet dies or even runs away, you realize it wasn't because your pet didn't care for you.

But when a relationship breaks up, it's different. The love and care that once existed for you is dried up. It's vanished into thin air. The other person still exists. You may still see each other from time to time, which makes it even more difficult.

Secondary Losses

As you experience the loss of this relationship, at first you experience the absence of the person. But every loss carries with it a series of secondary losses as well. And each of these must be identified, grieved over, and in some way let go. Think of the various losses you've experienced.

61

A while ago you were a couple. The couple relationship is now gone. The activities you shared are gone. Your schedule together may have included daily phone calls or Friday and Saturday date nights. All those rituals are gone. And you feel the emptiness. Your other losses could include

the interdependency you created

hopes and dreams for the future

your ex-partner's family members with whom you bonded

how you felt by having this person as a part of your life

gifts or affirmations you were accustomed to receiving

help you received on a regular basis from your ex

Often you leave some of your single friends behind as you invest more time and energy into this new relationship. It may not be intentional, it just happens. You may not think about it much because it takes place gradually as you experience the delight of a new relationship. You're also entering your partner's world and will make new friends. Your world becomes more and more of a couple's world.

But when the relationship ends, you're likely to feel a huge secondary loss. The newly acquired friends may not linger, so you're left with a void. Some of them may feel torn. You may have really clicked with some of them, but their initial loyalty was with your ex. What's more, the friends you had back when you were single may have forgotten about you.

I mention these secondary losses to make you aware of them. Often, in the aftermath of a breakup, one's vision is so clouded that it's difficult to see the many different losses. But because each of these losses needs to be grieved over, it's important to identify them.

How Long?

"Norm, how long? How long is this pain going to last? How long is it going to take for me to recover? When will the thoughts, the feelings, the memories go away so I can go on with my life?" I hear these questions frequently because I work with many people who are experiencing grief in some way over the loss of a relationship.

I'm not sure I can give you an exact answer, because the estimates vary. We do know, however, when you lose a close loved one in what is called a "normal" death, the average length of time for recovery is about two years. With an accidental death, it's three years.

The authors of *Letting Go,* a book about recovering from a broken heart, concluded that the average amount of time it takes for haunting memories to subside and for normal functioning to return was usually one half the duration of the relationship. This conclusion was based on interviews with those who suffer from depression, feelings of inadequacy, and loss of self-esteem. Their finding indicates it would take two years to recover from the loss of a four-year relationship, six years to recover from the loss of a twelve-year relationship, and so on. But the authors also say that the length of recovery time will vary according to the individual and the intensity of the relationship.[2]

Another pair of authors describes the emotional state of people who break up as "love shock," which is a mixture of numbness, disorientation, emptiness, and anxiety. It is similar to a crisis reaction or grieving over any kind of loss. They suggest it takes most people about a year to complete their "love shock" experience, but it's not unusual for the process to take longer.[3]

Here's a good rule of thumb: the more you learn how to cope with crisis and the more knowledgeable you are about grief, the faster you will be able to recover. Learning about grief and realizing that what you're experiencing is normal can lift some of your discomfort. And remember, don't try to go through this experience by yourself. We recover better when another person walks with us on the path of recovery.

You and your grief can't be pushed. There's no fast-forward button. You'll recover in stages with some periods of calm in between. Stabilizing your life involves acceptance of the fact that your life as you knew it for the last year or two or three will never be the same again. It also involves realizing that regardless of how you feel, you have a full life before you—a life full of purpose and meaning.

Others

Recovering from this loss will be a struggle, and you probably won't have the support that you want at this time. You may understand that your recovery will take time, even months, but many of those around you won't be patient with you. They'll prod you with questions and statements to get you back into the mainstream of life.

I know of one couple who broke up after six years. For them, it was a mutual decision with a minimal amount of pain. But it was a different story for their respective families and friends. They were all stunned; it was *their* lives that came to a standstill, and they gave the couple a lot of grief over the breakup.

One woman client said about her friends and family, "I felt as though I'd been excommunicated by life. After four years my ex and I weren't going anywhere. Jim was so nice and likeable, but if we'd married, I would be the initiator and he'd follow. I didn't want to be a mother to my husband. But the reaction from our friends! It's as though I've got leprosy. He was so close to our boss at the company, I wonder if I've even got a job anymore!"

Hopefully some close friends will listen to you and help you through your journey of grief, but well-meaning friends can also give you bad advice. Unfortunately, people love to give advice, even when they really don't know what they're talking about. Why? Because people really do want to help, and they want to feel valued. Most, however, won't give you good advice because they simply don't know the answers.

Be careful what you ask your friends. It doesn't help to ask them why they think the breakup happened. How would they know? They don't have all the facts, nor do they understand all the dynamics involved. Don't ask them what you should do or how to get the person back in your life. And remember, your friends are friends, not experts.

Often the breakup comes as a major shock to friends and family because while a couple is together, they often do their best to present a rosy picture of how things are between them. It's no surprise, then, that family members and friends are taken off guard when what they thought was a peaceful union suddenly goes up in smoke.

Alignments will occur. Some friends will support your ex, others will support you. The advantage is with the initiator here because he or she has more of an opportunity to develop a support network.[4] But the person who lost the relationship will need to develop a support network as well. This is one of the reasons why it's always important to have good friends outside of a romantic relationship.

The Fear of Loving Again

Some people face breakups squarely, learn from them, override their fears, and grow to trust and love again. But others allow their emotional wounds to remain open; they

65

give in to their fears by withdrawing from any future romantic relationships.

Nancy, a thirty-two-year-old, described how she felt: "Jim and I dated for two years. I really thought it was going somewhere. We'd had some discussions about the future. We even mentioned marriage. But one day we were a couple, the next I was single. There's so much I miss now. I miss his presence. He was enjoyable to have around. And we had a fairly regular pattern of seeing one another and doing things together. It was an enjoyable routine. And I thought we fit together fairly well.

"We were mentioned always as a couple. I'm not the only one shocked and upset over this breakup. My friends start to refer to us as a couple and then end up correcting themselves. It's embarrassing for all of us. I'm struggling with a lot, even with figuring out who I really am.

"If I only had to deal with the feelings of this breakup it would be a bit easier. But I've had two others. I thought I'd gotten over those all right. But that pain came back as well. So now I'm a third-time loser. Either I have the gift of picking the wrong men or I pick the right ones and they see defects in me that I'm blind to. Could I have been too cautious in this relationship because of the other experiences? I don't know. I just don't want this to happen again."

The fear that this could happen again is especially strong if there have been numerous breakups over the years. Once an intimate relationship ends, a part of you wants to try again with a new relationship. But as with Nancy, another part says, "Forget it. Don't do it! It isn't worth the risk!" You're afraid the past will recur, and a new relationship will end up the same way. Or you're afraid you will always feel the loss and pain of your previous breakup and will never be able to reach out and love again.

The fear of reliving the past paralyzes the normal process of building a new relationship. This fear creates a hesitation to invest energy, love, and transparency in a new love interest. Many people who are afraid to move ahead in a new relationship are also afraid to remain behind without anyone to love. They feel trapped between the fear of loving again and the fear that they will never be loved again. Additional emotions feed the fear of loving again. One of them is guilt—the feeling that you have failed yourself, your ideals, your Lord, or the other person. Sometimes you think, "I wasted all these years on that person." This guilt may exist whether you were the *rejected* person or the *rejecting* person. Unresolved guilt damages self-esteem, and low self-esteem produces greater fear. If you feel guilty about a broken relationship, it's important to identify whether the feelings are based on reality (such as breaking a commitment or acting irresponsibly toward the other person) or imagination (taking the blame for something that was not really your responsibility).

If you've experienced a lot of rejection in your life, your fear of being rejected again could cause you to behave in ways that bring about rejection. And many people are so down on themselves that they're their own worst enemies. They put themselves down, degrade themselves, dump on themselves, and rarely give themselves the benefit of the doubt. And since they don't like themselves, they project a negative picture of who they are to others.

But your concern now may be, "What do I do about my rejection? What about my fear of being rejected in the future?"

Remember there *is* hope. Your fear of rejection can diminish or vanish. It *is* possible, especially when your hope is in the person of Jesus Christ. That's how we begin to overcome *both* the effects of a relationship rejection and the fear of a future rejection. We need to experience the ultimate source of acceptance. We'll take a closer look at this later.

Anger

Expressions of anger have always been with us. We find anger expressed in the psalms and the books of the proph-

67

ets. Job expressed anger at God, as did Jonah and Elijah. Anger is a sign of protest—a reaction against something that shouldn't have happened. It's a way of fighting back when you feel helpless. And it is a normal response to feeling like you've been unjustly deprived of something valuable, in this case a relationship. At whom do we get angry most often? God. We blame him. He shouldn't have done this, or he shouldn't have allowed that. He's supposed to do things right, which means according to the way we want!

When you blame God, it's unnerving and unsettling to other people, so they either respond with Christian clichés or try to convince you that your anger at God is irrational. They fail to realize that nothing they say will help, because you're living on emotions at this point. Even though you may be raising questions, you're not really looking for answers.

The good news is that when anger is expressed to God, it can be analyzed, dealt with, and it can lead to a rediscovery of the character and purposes of God.

Our anger may also be directed toward other people, especially the ex-partner. It's not uncommon for ex-partners to badmouth each other. Sometimes ex-partners do this so much others wonder what the two of them ever saw in each other! Why does a rejected person begin to talk about their ex in such a negative manner? It's because of loss. You experience a loss when the other leaves. You hurt. You've been hurt. You tend to talk about the negative aspects of the person, so you can think of the loss as an *acceptable* loss. By focusing on the negative of what you leave behind, it's easier to walk away from it.[5]

Perhaps the initial step in overcoming anger with one's ex-partner is to take inventory of the hurts. One man wrote:

I was so angry at you for the lies.
I resent the fact that I have to change churches. It should be the other way around for what you did.
I feel wounded by your betrayal of me. We had talked about marriage, but you were straying even then.
I am angry that you took two years out of my life.

Often, when a person begins listing these resentments, buried hurts and feelings climb through the barriers. This list is for your own use and is not to be shared with anyone else except God. Making such a list is *not* an easy experience.

After you've made your list, go into a room and set up two chairs facing each other. Sit in one chair and imagine the other person sitting opposite you, listening to what you are sharing. Read your list aloud with your tone and inflections reflecting the feelings you have. Don't be concerned about editing what you are saying. Just get it out.

Some people keep their list for days, adding to it as things come to mind. Others find it helpful to sit down and share like this several times for the benefits of multiple episodes of emotional drainage. Don't be surprised to find yourself feeling angry, depressed, intense, embarrassed, or anxious. When you have concluded your time of sharing, spend a few minutes in prayer sharing these feelings with God, thanking him for understanding what you are experiencing and for his presence in your life to help you overcome the feelings.

Sometimes our anger is vented toward anyone who is around, especially family members. You may get angry at those who fail to reach out and support you during this time.

When we hurt, we want to be acknowledged. We don't want people to pretend everything is okay, because it isn't. And in some cases it never will be the same.

You may direct your anger inward. Women are more likely to do this, while men generally turn anger outward. Often anger comes because we feel out of control, powerless, and victimized.

How do you deal with anger in a positive way? You admit it, you accept it, you release it in a healthy way. A friend of mine wrote the following poem. Maybe you can relate.

I Told God I Was Angry

I told God I was angry. I thought He'd be surprised.
I thought I'd kept hostility quite cleverly disguised.

I told the Lord I hate Him. I told Him that I hurt.
I told Him that He isn't fair, He treated me like dirt.

I told God I was angry but *I'm* the one surprised.
"What I've known all along," He said, "you've finally realized."

"At last you have admitted what's really in your heart.
Dishonesty, not anger, was keeping us apart."

"Even when you hate Me I don't stop loving you.
Before you can receive that love you must confess what's true."

"In telling me the anger you genuinely feel,
It loses power over you, permitting you to heal."

I told God I was sorry and He's forgiven me.
The truth that I was angry has finally set me free.

There's Hope

Before ending this chapter, I'd like to tell you about a woman who came into my office the second week after the breakup of her four-year relationship. She said, "I'm just not myself. I'm doing things I've never done before and I just hate it. I wouldn't want anyone to know how irrational I am right now. You know what I've done this week? I can't believe it. I followed cars and even people that I thought were my ex. Of course they weren't. I've also called some mutual friends to find out subtly whether they've heard anything or talked to my ex or if he's seeing anyone. I guess I wasn't that subtle either.

"Yesterday I drove to my ex's work and apartment. I called from pay phones, so the number couldn't be traced. I just wanted to hear his voice. I know it's over, but I keep hoping. I have some of his things, but if I send them back, it will seem so final. I keep hoping even though I know it's over. When I think of all that wasted time, I get a pain in my stomach. I've had a headache, can't eat, and when I do, it doesn't stay with me . . . what's wrong with me?"

Nothing was wrong. All that she said is part of a normal response. When you lose someone significant, you don't want to let them go, so you hang on in any way that you can. You do what you think is irrational, and this makes you think you're going crazy. These acts of desperation are only a problem if they persist.

For many, a breakup is a crisis. It's a time when you've been thrown off balance, you're confused, can't think straight, and your emotions are in disarray. What you want most is relief. But there's something else. A breakup is a time when you'll make some of the greatest changes in your life. You will come out of it a better, stronger person than you were before.

Now that we've identified what it's like to go through the initial stages of a breakup, let's consider the process of recovery.

5

Making the Best of It

So, how do I recover? The first thing to do is face what has happened to you. You may not like what happened, but accepting it does not mean liking it. If you deny you're in pain, you're stuck.

You will hurt. Pain is the natural result of loss, especially when a dream dies. When there's a hole in your life, pain fills it for a time. This is normal. If you didn't feel this pain, you would be like the leper who can't feel his hand burning in a blazing fire.

Time: A Precious Commodity

You probably have a timetable for recovery, and if you're like most, it is not realistic. You'd like to be over the pain right now—today—this moment. Instant recovery simply does not happen in real life. There's no quick fix for emotional pain. A big part of your life and even your identity has been cut off. And contrary to what other people might have you believe, this is not a minor injury, it's a deep, serious wound. Dick Innes, in *How to Mend a Broken Heart,* says

> Nature has its own time schedule. You can't push it. A scratch heals in a few days. A broken bone takes six weeks. You can't speed either one up, but you can take good care of the wound, doing what you can to facilitate its healing and letting nature take its course by giving it the time it requires to heal.
>
> The same principle applies to healing wounds of the heart. You can't speed up the process, but you can stop it from taking longer than necessary—by taking good care of yourself, doing what you can to facilitate your healing, and giving yourself permission to take time to heal.[1]

The recovery time of a breakup is directly related to three factors:

1. How long you were involved in the relationship
2. How close the two of you were
3. How you perceive the chances of finding someone else[2]

Obviously, the first factor is that the longer a person had been with her ex-partner, the longer she would need to recover. But what about the second factor? How can a person tell how "close" he was to his ex-partner? The longer you were involved, the closer you were likely to be. You had more shared experiences and perhaps more dreams that have now been shattered. As for the third, if you think you'll never find someone else, you'll end up feeling stuck.

After breaking up it's best not to think about future relationships for a while. That will come later.

People experience a lot of confusion at the beginning of the grieving process, so be patient. Don't take action. Push the delay button. Write out your feelings. Write out your prayers. If it's a difficult day, call a friend and ask them to pray for you. Above all, do not begin any new relationships for several months or as long as it takes to recover. After all, would you want to begin a relationship with someone who was mourning over a former partner?

Getting over a breakup is in many ways like a car that has stalled and needs to sit awhile before it moves on. Years ago, when cars had the old-style carburetor, there would be a vapor lock. This shut down the engine and you just had to wait. The engine didn't need a major overhaul or even a minor tune up. It just needed to cool down until it got back to normal. And it did. Just like you will. While you wait, please remember: Your options are *not* closed. As this door closes, many new ones open.

Cleaning Up Memory Lane

You've got to want to let go of your past life with this person. Our emotions and their intensity are related to memory, and there are different variations of memory. As Henri Nouwen put it, "Remorse is a biting memory, guilt is an accusing memory, gratitude is a joyful memory and all such emotions are deeply influenced by the way we have integrated past events into our way of being in the world. In fact, we perceive our world with our memories."[3] What are *your* memories right now?

Have you ever considered the possibility that much of the suffering of a person's life comes from memories? The reason they hurt is because they tend to be mostly buried and emerge only when they choose. The more painful these memories are, the more hidden and repressed they become. They hide, as it were, in a corner of the deepest cavern of our minds. Because they are hidden, they go unhealed.

When a relationship is over, what you have left are the memories. A common response when there's a loss of this type is to idealize the person you lost. You think only of the positive qualities that you are going to miss rather than being objective. Keep in mind the more you idealize the person, the longer your recovery is delayed. Some have found it helpful to complete a Relationship Balance Sheet, which consists of a list of "positives" about the relationship beside a list of "problems." Why not take some time to fill out a Relationship Balance Sheet right now?

Positives	Problems
1.	1.
2.	2.
3.	3.
4.	4.
5.	5.
6.	6.
7.	7.
8.	8.
9.	9.
10.	10.

When it comes to a failed relationship, many people end up listing more problems than positives, and it is important for a person who is mourning the end of a relationship to see this.

What do you do with a painful memory? You may try to forget it, or you may act as though it did not occur. Trying to forget the pains of the past gives these memories power and control over your life, and you proceed through life dragging weight. You attempt to edit your own personal history by choosing what to remember and what to forget, but there is a twofold cost: you continue to limp through life, and you miss out on an opportunity to grow and mature.

It doesn't have to be this way. A painful memory can be transformed into a blessing, but the first step is to face the memory. Again, Henri Nouwen: "What is forgotten is unavailable and what is unavailable cannot be healed."[4] When you face each memory, ask yourself, "Why was this a problem? Why was this painful? What did I or can I learn from this experience?" This is a way to put the memory to rest. I've known some who have written good-bye letters to each memory and then read the letter aloud. This can be a wonderful way to let go of painful memories.

Placing a Down Payment on Your Emotional Debt

From time to time we all accrue emotional debt—when we trap feelings inside and block off our capacity to feel. But the more we create a barrier around our feelings, the more constricted we become. Hurt is a part of life. Being let down is a part of life. Being rejected is a part of life. We live in an imperfect world, so getting hurt is bound to happen from time to time.

Getting out of emotional debt involves accepting yourself and others, shortcomings and all. If you are guarding your emotional life, you're under continual stress, and your vision of reality is clouded. No matter how painful your past experiences have been, no matter how much you want to remain at a safe intellectual distance from your pain, healthy people need both to think and feel.

People who stuff their feelings often detach themselves from others. This detachment is born out of fear, and these people live in constant fear. For them, fear is like a soft hum in their ears, reminding them to be cautious and wary.

If any of this is hitting close to home, consider these questions. What is it you are afraid of? What is the worst possible thing that could happen to you if you opened your life to your feelings? Would it be any worse than what you are experiencing now?

If you want to live life in the present, with hope for the future, accept what has happened in the past, for it cannot be changed. If you are lonely, share your feelings with someone. If you are sad, tell someone. By doing so you'll be placing a down payment on your emotional debt.

Your Children

When a family with children dissolves because of a divorce, the family that the children knew dies. If you have children, you're well aware of the experience. Fortunately, more attention is being given to the impact of divorce on children. Unfortunately, very little is given to the impact of a parent's breakup on children. Their sense of loss is rarely addressed. But in some cases a breakup can be even more devastating than a divorce. Consider the following situations.

When Jimmy was a year and a half old, his parents divorced. He really didn't feel the impact because the divorce happened so early that Jimmy was accustomed to seeing his father two weekends a month and during an extended stay in the summer. It was just normal. When he was three, however, his mother began dating a man who spent a great amount of time at Jimmy's house. He visited three or four evenings a week and many hours on the weekend. Jimmy and he became very close. When Jimmy was six, his mother broke off this relationship and began dating another man. Jimmy was crushed.

Born out of wedlock, Fred never had a father. But when he was seven, his mom brought home a man named Steve.

Steve became the first "father" he'd ever had. Two years later Steve broke off the relationship and never said good-bye to Fred. He felt rejected and abandoned and wondered what he had done wrong. Subsequently, he closed himself off to other men his mother dated and wouldn't give them the time of day.

Your child's responses to your breakup may include sadness, abandonment, isolation, confusion, disorientation, and anger. When you date, your child will compare the new person in your life with the old person, share family secrets with him or her, and perhaps tell your ex-partner about the two of you. Your child may resist your efforts to have an ongoing relationship with this individual and may take steps to sabotage your dreams to have a life with this new individual.

In many cases, because your child has lost one parental figure, he or she could be especially needy, quickly attaching to new partners of yours. Just remember, *the greater the attachment, the greater the loss when there's a breakup.* You might be glad a relationship is over and feel little grief. But your child could be crushed. If you don't allow and help them to grieve this loss (and it will take longer than you think and want), there will be long-term damage. Don't leave your children out of the picture. Talk with them, listen, reflect, and be patient. Help them grieve by taking some of the steps you've taken.

Grief Defined and Explained

Grieving is an active process of confronting loss and doing what needs to be done with it to move on with life. When you live in denial, however, you push anything unpleasant out of your life. In denial you passively float down a river of pain but at the same time you don't admit the pain is there. You're floating along often at the mercy of the current. Grieving admits and faces the pain. It sets a course, notes the currents and rapids in the river, and paddles through it all to maintain its course. Grief is *not* despair. Grief feels and deals with loss. Despair is a sense of futility—the idea that nothing can be done to get out of this. It's a passive resignation and it grinds you into hopelessness.[5] When grief enters your life, you enter a valley—a valley of shadows. There is nothing pleasant about grief. It's painful. It's work. It's a lingering process. But it's necessary for healing.

Grief brings many changes. It appears differently at various times, and it flits in and out of your life. It's natural, normal, predictable, and should be expected when your relationship is over. Don't let anyone say something is wrong with you. Grieving is not an abnormal response to a breakup. In fact, just the opposite is true. The *absence* of grief is abnormal. Grief is your own personal experience and does not have to be accepted or validated by others.[6]

Bundle of Emotions

There is a bundle of emotions involved in the grieving process, emotions that seem out of control and in conflict with one another. At different times you may experience bitterness, emptiness, apathy, love, anger, guilt, sadness, fear, self-pity, and helplessness.

During your time of grief and recovery, you'll experience a jumbled mess of feelings that will leave you wondering, "Am I normal or crazy?" This in itself is normal and to be expected.

One minute you're confused and the next you've got it all together. Confusion will be a companion that comes and goes. You'll be sentimental at times, especially as thoughts and mementos trigger your sadness. Your feelings will surge back and forth like a wave coming into shore and out again. You're likely to vacillate from dwelling on your partner to blocking out all thoughts.

Other Effects

With grief your entire body experiences it—feelings, thoughts, and attitudes. It impacts you socially as you interact with others. You experience it physically as it affects your health and is expressed in bodily symptoms. If you wonder where that migraine came from or why your stomach is off, ask your grief.

Letting Go

One of the biggest steps of the grieving process is letting go of your ex. Dick Innes told this story of two monks returning home to their abbey:

> It was a dismal, rainy day. On rounding a bend on the way, they came to a swollen stream which was threatening to overflow its banks. Standing by the stream was a beautiful woman too nervous to chance the flooded crossing for fear she might get swept away.
>
> "Allow me to carry you across the stream," said one of the monks, as he picked her up and carried her safely to the other side.
>
> Later that night the other monk suddenly blurted out, "I think you made a grave mistake today picking up that woman. You know we are not to have any dealings with the opposite sex."
>
> "How strange," remarked the monk. "I carried her across the stream. You are carrying her still."

Unfortunately, many grieving people are still carrying the person they lost.[7]

What does letting go in a relationship mean? Here are several possibilities:

81

1. It means making a clear and firm decision to end your involvement with memories. After you've faced them, felt the pain, said good-bye, and released them, it's time to move on.
2. It means taking responsibility for the decision to let go and knowing that it is the right thing to do.
3. It means making a promise to yourself that the relationship *is* over.
4. It means making it clear to your ex-partner by your actions that it's over.
5. It means sticking by this decision, no matter how painful the process.

Guard yourself; be sure you stay away from your ex-partner. Any thoughts you have of getting him or her to take you back need to be dropped. I've seen some plead and beg for a partner to come back. This is where the rational part of you needs to override your emotions. Think about it: would you really want to be with someone whom you had to prod into a relationship with you? Would you want to go through life telling others, "Aren't I the fortunate one? I talked him into accepting me and taking me back as his partner." I don't know anyone who would, and I doubt you would either.

If you run into the other person socially, don't cower and hide or slink away. Be pleasant, positive, and brief. If your ex wants to stay and talk or explain more, don't. Give yourself permission to say no, talk with someone else, or leave the room. You need your space, your separateness, and your self-esteem.

When it comes to letting the past go, you have three choices. Even though it's impossible to go back and relive your life, I know a number of people who have made the choice to live in the past rather than the present. They never let go of it and thus can't move forward.

Others I've seen deal with their pain and resolve it but are so scared that they stay where they are, stuck, and still don't move ahead.

You have another choice. Once you've let go of the past, you can move ahead; take wisdom-based risks, be willing to love again. Someone said life can only be understood by looking backward, it must be lived by looking forward.[8] God's purpose for your life is not in your past but in your future and to go ahead you'll need to grieve.

Why Grief?

Why do people suffering from a breakup have to go through this experience? What's the purpose? Keep these things in mind:

Through grief you express your feelings of loss.

Through grief you express your anger with the loss as well as your desire to change what happened.

Through grief you express your feelings about the effects of the loss.[9]

The purpose of grieving is to get *beyond* these reactions, so you can move on with your life. Grief is to bring you to the point of making necessary changes, so you can live with the loss in a healthy way. It's a matter of beginning with the question, "Why did this have to happen to me?" and moving to, "How can I learn through this experience? How can I now go on with my life?" When the "How?" question replaces the "Why?" question, you have started to live with the reality of the loss. "Why?" questions reflect a search for meaning and purpose in loss. "How?" questions reflect your search for ways to adjust to the loss.[10]

In the next chapter we'll look at the ins and outs, the actual "work" of grieving.

The Work of Grieving
Stages 1, 2, and 3

In the last chapter we talked about several things one must go through on the way to recovery after a breakup—giving yourself time, cleaning up memory lane, letting go, grieving. Before considering the work of grieving, take a moment to reflect on where you are in your recovery journey. Perhaps you're just starting, or maybe you're nearing the end. Just remember, you can't bypass the process without doing yourself harm—you must go through it.

Let's consider how to move through this process. Like the grief experienced when a person dies, the stages you will go through to recover from a lost relationship are predictable. These stages constitute the normal and healthy process of grieving. If the healing is complete, you will have some emotional scars but no emotional wounds. I've talked to people who still have open sores from a relationship that ended fifteen years ago. That's sad and it doesn't have to be that way. Keep in mind that the stages I mention here vary in length and intensity according to the particulars of each case.

Usually there are six stages you will go through when a love relationship falls apart. The bad news is your pain will be the greatest during the first three stages, which are the stages covered in this chapter. The good news is as you move through each stage, the intensity of pain diminishes. The further along the path you proceed, the less fear you will experience. What you want to avoid is getting *stuck* in a stage and not completing the process; this can cripple your future involvements.

Some of these stages overlap, and you may move back and forth between them for a while. This is normal and should be accepted as part of the healing process.

Stage 1: Shock

The initial stage is *shock,* which was mentioned earlier. When you first lose a love relationship, you're dumbfounded. You're overwhelmed by shock. Even when the breakup or divorce has been anticipated, the reality of it has a unique effect. Some are unable to carry on their day-to-day activities. Even eating and sleeping are chores. You live by your feelings at this stage, even though you feel numb.

Whether or not you can identify it, you're likely to experience an intense fear of being alone forever. Remember, you need to experience these feelings in order to move through the healing process. At this stage you need safe, accepting people around you, whether or not you feel like having them around. The presence of other people can help ease the fear of loneliness. They can listen and reflect back to you what you're feeling and saying.

Stage 2: Grief

The second stage is *grief*. The grief stage may be extensive because it includes mourning the loss of what you shared together and what you *could have* shared together. The words of Billy Sprague following the death of his fiancée are relevant:

> I moved to a vacant lot, at least emotionally. All the dreams and plans and longings were leveled to the horizon and beyond. The season in my heart changed to winter and refused to allow spring to come for over two years.
>
> In my experience, the landscape ahead was shrouded in uncertainty. I couldn't see one day ahead of me. I became a foot watcher, walking through airports or the grocery store staring at my feet, methodically moving through a misty world. One foot, then the other. . . . I came to associate faith with simply tying my shoes. Some days, especially early on, it was the only act of faith I could muster.[1]

During this time, you're hit by seasons of sadness, depression, anger, calm, fear, and eventually hope, but they don't follow one another progressively. They overlap, often chaotically. Just when you think you're over one emotion, it comes barging through your door again. You finally smile, but then the tears return. You laugh, but the cloud of depression drifts in once again. This is normal. This is necessary. This is healing.

A healthy response to a loss involves feelings of depression after the initial shock wears off. Surprising? Some losses are *very* painful, and a depressive response is normal. The depression is there for a purpose: to help us experience the loss and to recover from it. Depression begins to develop, and the depth of it depends on the intensity of attachment you had to your ex. Eventually the depression levels out and we begin to recover.

But the person who has had excessive losses in his or her life and has never learned to grieve may have developed negative patterns of thinking. These destructive thought patterns may cause him to hold on to the loss or continually re-create it. Pessimism continues to re-create a loss. Some people have been taught, "Don't hope and you won't be disappointed" or "Expect the worst and protect yourself." This is one of the ways to create the "runaway train" syndrome of depression. Leaving a train parked on a downgrade without the brake properly set leads to some predictable consequences. As the train moves down the tracks, it picks up momentum and is soon out of control.

Manifestations of pessimism, which allow depression to gather this momentum, include guilt, self-blame, negative self-talk, distortions of reality, misperceptions, and imagining additional losses. The depression becomes self-perpetuating because we give it fuel.

As the weeks go by after the breakup, there are steps you can take to lessen your sadness or depression and begin to recover. When a person seems stuck in their "relationship loss," it helps to look for what triggers your sadness. Of the many causes we often find two about which you can do something.

First, it may help to identify places the two of you went— places that, if you went to them now, would make you sad. Avoiding such places is one option. I have talked to people who have changed jobs, avoided restaurants, what used to be favorite recreational haunts, and even churches because they were painful reminders of what used to be. But this is allowing the other person to control and dominate your life.

Another option is purposely going back to these places by yourself (*a*) to say good-bye to them as places you visited when you were a member of a couple and (*b*) to claim them for your own as an individual. Take a close friend or relative with you, and go back to the restaurant or favorite haunt. Make it a special time and ask God's blessing on the location and the occasion. The more you stay away, the greater your fear will be. By returning, you dilute the pain. In time, when it comes to memories that are associated with these places, you can move from emotional flashback to historical reminiscence.

Secondly, if you both work at the same place or attend the same church, it is especially important for you to take charge of the sadness, otherwise you may end up letting the breakup dictate where you work and worship. Tell yourself you're feeling sad, it's all right to feel this way, it's normal for what you've experienced, and in time it will diminish.

A young friend of mine who recently went through a breakup said that one of the most restorative things he heard came from his mother. She told him that as far as she was concerned, his ex had lost the greatest thing ever to come into her life. Why was this helpful? It was helpful because it reminded my friend that he was a valuable person despite his self-talk to the contrary. If you're constantly beating up on yourself as a result of this breakup—feeling worthless and just plain crummy—remember that you are a person of inestimable value. You are a cherished treasure of God himself. It might be a good idea for you to ask someone you trust to tell you the things he or she appreciates about you. It may sound corny, but believe me, when you're down, it's good for the soul.

The pain from a loss creates additional feelings, a frequent example of which is anxiety. Anxiety is fear of pain in the future. Some people experience potential tragedy so clearly in their thoughts, the dread that comes upon them can be as strong as if it had really occurred. Anxiety can be beneficial if you ask yourself what you are afraid of and why it is so important to you. Then you can take steps to prevent or minimize future hurt.

Some people become experts with mental gymnastics during the grief stage. These are mental games or tricks that we employ to deny, avoid, or defer an experience of loss. We attempt to shield ourselves from the pain, but we never defeat the enemy through these efforts. We simply prolong its accompanying pain.

Anxiety is fear of pain in the future.

This is also when certain "myths" rear their heads. One of these is "Nobody understands." This myth says your situation is so unique it's inconceivable to think anyone else could understand. It is important to realize that those who have gone through heartbreak do understand every aspect of it. They understand the feeling of abandonment, self-blame, other-blame, anger, guilt, and the knifelike anguish.

Many experience mild paranoia. Thoughts like "Everyone is talking about me," "I'm the subject of their conversations," "They're avoiding me," and "No one wants to be around me," come frequently to mind, especially if the breakup is the end of an office romance. Unfortunately, people who have been through a breakup often believe these thoughts, and worse yet, in some narrow, unloving churches, they are true.

Obsessive thinking is another regular part of the grieving stage. Do any of the following relate to your past or present life?

You arrange "accidental meetings" with the other person.

You listen for the telephone and run for it when it rings.

You listen to sad songs and think they are about you and the one you lost.

You think you see your former love or his or her car everywhere.

You want to contact the person but you're afraid of rejection.

You spend a great amount of time thinking about the person, devising plans of what to say or how to get him or her back.

You just know that this relationship was the best one you could ever have.

What other thoughts do you have? Perhaps it would help to make a list of them and take steps to put them to rest.[2]

1.
2.
3.
4.
5.

Sometimes when you've been dumped, you have difficulty freeing your mind from thinking about your ex. If you still have contact with him or her, you may want to keep what is referred to as a *bankbook*.

This is a special notebook that you use exclusively for writing down things you want to say to your ex. These could be questions, rebuttals, promises, apologies, or things you wished you had said at the time of breakup. In the process of writing these statements you may decide you don't need to say certain things after all. On the other hand, if you do need to say them, when you talk to your ex, you won't have to worry about forgetting what to say. Here are several other good reasons for keeping such a book:

It will save you the embarrassment of contacting the person when you have a thought you feel you need to share. Share it with your bankbook first and decide a month later whether to share it with your ex.

By keeping a bankbook of statements, you don't need to carry them around in your mind.

By writing your thoughts, you cut down the time you spend on them. In doing this you will learn how to limit your memories and thoughts to briefer and briefer periods of time each day until eventually you no longer think much at all about your ex.[3]

If you're not going to see or talk to your ex again but are struggling with the same thoughts, I recommend writing down what you would say, if you could, and reading your words to an empty chair.

"Thought stopping" is another necessary step in the grieving process. This is when you take a look at each of your thoughts and consider them as rationally and objectively as possible. Following this paragraph are the negative thoughts of a woman who went through a breakup alongside the answers she used to counter her negative thoughts. You may find it beneficial to monitor and chart your own thoughts in this way.

Negative Thoughts	Answers
He shouldn't have left me for another woman.	I don't like it, but he should have left because he did. For all the reasons I don't know of, he should have left. I don't have to like it, just accept it.
I need him.	I want him back, but I don't need him. I need

	food, water, and shelter to survive. I don't need a man to survive. Thinking in terms of "needs" makes me vulnerable.
This always happens to me, and it will never change.	Just because it happened in one case doesn't mean it has happened or will happen in every case.
This is terrible, awful, horrible.	These are labels I add to the facts. The labels don't change anything, and they make me feel worse.
I must have someone to love me.	It's nice to love and be loved, but making it a condition to happiness is a way of putting myself down.
I'm too ugly and too fat to find anyone else.	"Too" is a relative concept, not some absolute standard. Thinking like this is self-defeating and stops me from trying.
I can't stand being alone.	I can stand difficulties—as I have in the past. I just don't like them.
I made a fool out of myself.	There's no such thing as a fool. This mislabeling doesn't do me any good and makes me feel bad.
He made me depressed.	No one can make me feel depressed. I make myself depressed by the way I'm thinking.[4]

Even if you have thoughts that return again and again, there is hope. They *can* be done away with. First, pray out loud, sharing your concern, and describe specifically what you want God to do with these thoughts. Second, read aloud the following passages, which talk about how we can control our thought life: Isaiah 26:3; Ephesians 4:23; Colossians 3:1–2; 2 Corinthians 10:5; and Philippians 4:6–9. Identify one of the most persistent or upsetting thoughts, the one that pops into your head more frequently than the others. Now select a time when you're not upset. Say the thought in the form of a statement out loud without crying or becoming angry. If you can't, that's all right. In time, you will be able to do this. When you say the last word of the statement, slam a book or ruler loudly on a table or just clap your hands. Here's an example: "How could she have been so deceptive and *unfair?*"

Repeat the sentence again and again, each time moving the emphasis back one word. In time, this thought will be interrupted before it has a chance to be sad. And as this happens, thank God for taking this thought from your life.[5]

Stage 3: Blame

You may hold feelings of blame and anger toward your former partner—or even toward yourself. Your behavior during this stage may surprise you as you attempt to rid yourself of these feelings. Your actions may not seem to fit your past patterns. You may engage in compulsive behaviors such as shopping or eating binges, alcohol abuse, or even promiscuity. It is not unusual for people to make poor decisions at this stage. The fear of rejection, isolation, or personal inadequacy prompts some people to violate their own value systems.

Jim was a thirty-five-year-old, whose girlfriend broke up with him to marry her employer. Jim was devastated by this, but gradually he began to date again. However, he was unsuccessful in the new relationship.

One day he explained, "I guess I'm still angry at her for leaving me. But there's no way I can make her pay for what she did to me, and I can't take my anger out on her. So that's probably why these new relationships aren't working out. I like the women I date, but I don't treat them well. I get angry at them, and I'm often rude. That's just not me! I guess I'm trying to get back at my ex by taking my anger out on these other women. And that's not good for them or for me. I guess I try to hurt them first because I'm afraid they may hurt me the way Sue did. And I don't ever want to be hurt like that again!"

The fear of rejection, isolation, or personal inadequacy prompts some people to violate their own value systems.

Fortunately, Jim had the insight to figure out what he was doing, and eventually he moved out of this stage.

During the grief and blame stages, some common mistakes can block your recovery. Generalizing after any broken relationship is so easy to do. You take one isolated belief or experience and make it apply to life in general. Time and again I've heard my counselees say, "All women are money minded," "All men are losers," "All men are sex animals," "All women are hysterics. They can't think." Such generalizations immobilize.

Another frequent mistake is falling into the trap of living by a self-fulfilling prophecy. Perhaps you've heard or even said, "I'll never find anyone else. I'm stuck in life. I'll always be single now." This belief blinds us from seeing any possibilities around us. It gives us the attitude and look of defeat, which serves to repel others from us.

95

These prophecies do nothing but undermine and cripple relationships.

Another mistake we tend to make after a broken relationship is a set of unrealistic expectations. We use words like *should* and *must*. When things don't happen according to our rigid set of beliefs, we perpetuate a life of disappointment. We use expectations for ourselves and for other people, expectations like

"I have to be perfect for anyone to love me."

"If I don't meet all his needs, he won't love me."

"If she cares about me, she will . . . and she won't . . ."

"If he reminds me of my former spouse or dating partner, he's not worth being with."

One of the most destructive responses to a breakup is when a person is unable to look at himself or herself. One day a man in my office made the statement, "Norm, I can't bear to face myself after what's happened in my life." Sometimes these people are best referred to as "runners." They're continually on the go. They do things to avoid having to deal with their situations and their feelings. They don't want to face themselves. Diversions include incessant working, playing, being out each night, sleeping, watching TV, and worse yet experimenting with alcohol and drugs. The frantic, hectic, busy life is just as bad as a withdrawn, lethargic existence.

A common mistake made in an attempt both to overcome the pain of loss and to strike back is "revenge loving." The hurt person plunges into a new relationship prematurely out of anger. This revenge could manifest itself in three different variations.

One is to engage in a new relationship simply to make the old partner jealous. People spend great amounts of energy in this approach because arrangements are made so the ex will see the new couple. Another variation is acting out toward the new person in your life the way you were treated by your former partner. If abuse was part of the previous relationship and you were the victim, the tables are now turned. If manipulation was the pattern, in order not to be hurt again this becomes your weapon and defense. A final variation of revenge loving is when an individual develops a relationship in which he or she is in control, so no one can ever hurt him or her again. In all three cases, both the revenge lover and the new person end up hurt, unhappy, and dissatisfied.

In one of his articles on forgiveness, Lewis Smedes said resentment punishes us more than the other person because most often the other individual isn't aware of the intensity of our feelings.

Remember when you looked through a magnifying glass at a spider or some ferocious bug? It looked so large and threatening! Magnification is yet another of the traps into which people fall after a broken relationship. You begin to think about the person you lost and are convinced he is having the time of his life, while you are living in despair and discouragement. You feel limited and constrained, while you are sure your ex is living life to the fullest.

I've heard both rejecters *and* rejectees make this statement: "That person really had a lot of problems and defects. She wasn't who or what she said she was. In the long run I think it's better that I look around and find someone else." For rejecters, the statement is a rationalization for why they broke off the relationship. For rejectees, it is a means of deadening the pain of the loss. For both, the statement contains elements of denial, and denial always delays recovery.

Where are you in these first three stages? If you skipped any, I suggest returning for a visit. In the end you'll be glad you did.

The Work of Grieving

Stages 4, 5, and 6

Life is full of good-byes. Some are for a brief time like when a child or spouse says good-bye before leaving for a day's activities. Other good-byes are permanent. These good-byes are declarations that something is over and a new time has come.

Saying good-bye is a significant part of your recovery, and this chapter's purpose is to help you say good-bye to your past relationship. Saying good-bye is when you really finally admit to yourself, "The relationship is over; this person is out of my life, and I have to go on." I have seen numerous people get stuck on the threshold of saying good-bye, sometimes for more than a year. Some of these people seem to move ahead, yet three weeks later they are asking the same questions and making the same statements about a reconciliation that will never happen. They are unwilling to say the final good-bye.

Let's look at the last three stages of grieving, which will help you say good-bye to your broken relationship and all the pain that came with it.

Stage 4: Forgiveness

To become a free person and move forward in life, there is an additional step involved in your recovery. It's called forgiveness. No one can tell you when it will happen. You can't hurry it, for it too is a process that takes time.

Most of us have our own set of reasons for not forgiving another person. We object to letting him or her off the hook, as it were. One of the ways to allow forgiveness to have a place in your life is to identify the objections you have to forgiving the person who hurt you so much.

Take a blank sheet of paper and write a salutation at the top. Use the name of your former partner: "Dear _____." Underneath the salutation, write the words, "I forgive you for _____." Then complete the sentence by stating something your ex did that still hurts and angers you. Then write down the first thought that comes to mind after writing the sentence. It may be a feeling or thought that actually contradicts the forgiveness you are trying to express. It may be an emotional rebuttal or protest to what you have just written. Keep writing the "I forgive you for . . ." statements for every thought or feeling that comes to the surface.

Your list may fill a page or even two. Don't be discouraged if your angry protests contradict the concept of forgiveness or are so firm and vehement that it seems as if you have not expressed any forgiveness at all. You are in

100

the process of forgiving this person, so keep writing until all the pockets of resentment have been drained. Once again, show this list to no one, but using an empty chair, read the list aloud as though the person were sitting there listening to you.

To follow is a sample of what a woman wrote to her former boyfriend who led her on for four years. The left column is her letter, the right column are the thoughts she wrote down after each "I forgive you for . . ." statement.

Dear Jim,

I forgive you for not being willing to share your feelings with me.

No, I don't. I still feel cheated by you. You were one way when we started dating and then changed.

I forgive you for withdrawing from me when I wanted to talk about our relationship.

I am still angry over your silence.

I forgive you for not trying to make our relationship work.

Why couldn't you have tried more? We might have made it!

I forgive you for sitting around watching TV when I wanted to go out and have fun.

It's still hard for me to understand why you didn't want to be with me.

I forgive you for the times you said I was just like your mother.

I guess there may have been some times when I acted the way she did. If only you had shared that with me earlier.

I forgive you for upsetting my life so much with this breakup.

I have trouble forgiving you for this. I don't think it had to be this way.

101

After she identified these as her main hurts, she continued to write these "forgiveness statements" each day for a week until she had no more rebuttals or complaints. When that happens, forgiveness is beginning.

Another way to do this is to take just one of the items of resentment and write it again and again on the paper, listing every rebuttal that comes to mind until you can say, "I forgive you for . . ." statements several times without any objection coming to mind. This will move you from living in the past to living in the present.

There are a number of things forgiveness isn't. It's not saying a simple okay. Think about it. What does okay mean? "You didn't hurt me. You didn't do anything wrong. You didn't offend me." When you've been betrayed or dumped, if you were hurt, you have some negative feelings toward the other. If the other person did something that was wrong, say it was wrong.

Forgiveness is not automatically restoring a relationship or having a casual friendship. Forgiveness does *not* mean going back to the way things were before. Eventually, you may end up with a casual friendship, but you may not. You may end up in the long run with a meaningful relationship, but you may not. These things can't be pushed or predicted. Sometimes all you can hope for is the ability on both your parts to say hello without a feeling of hurt or awkwardness. And again, this may or may not happen.

Forgiveness is not a complete forgetting. In time you will remember the events historically (i.e., factually) and not emotionally. If you say, "Oh, I've forgotten it already," you're probably in denial. You have to remember in order to learn from the experience. The memory may remain forever, but the hurt will diminish.[1]

When it comes to forgiveness, one of our problems is that most of us have better memories than God does. We cling to our hurts and nurse them, which causes us to experience difficulty with others or ourselves. When we don't forgive, it not only fractures our relationship with others but with God as well.

Is it fair to be stuck to a painful past? No! Is it fair to be walloped again and again by the same old hurt? No! But vengeance is like having a videotape planted inside your mind that can't be turned off. It plays that painful scene over and over. It hooks you into its instant replays like a ball game. Each time it replays, you feel the pain again. Do you really want to relive the pain again and again? Of course not. Listen: forgiveness is the turn-off button for the videotape of painful memories.[2]

When it comes to forgiveness, one of our problems is that most of us have better memories than God does.

Failing to forgive means inflicting inner torment upon yourself. When we reinforce internal messages that torment us by resisting forgiveness, we make ourselves miserable and ineffective. Forgiveness is saying, "It is all right, it is over. I no longer resent you or see you as an enemy. I love you, even if you cannot love me back."

When you forgive someone for hurting you, you perform spiritual surgery inside your soul; you cut away the cancer that's been eating away at you (resentment) and see your ex with new eyes. Detach that person from the hurt he or she caused you and let the hurt go.

Then invite your ex back into your mind, fresh, as if a piece of history between you had been erased, its grip on your memory broken. This is how you can reverse the seemingly irreversible flow of pain within you.[3]

We can forgive because God has forgiven us. He has given us a beautiful model of forgiveness. Allowing God's forgiveness to permeate our lives and renew us is the first step toward wholeness.

In response to the question, "How do you know when you have forgiven a person?" Lewis Smedes said you have forgiven a person when in your heart you begin to wish that person well. When we can pray for that person and ask for God's blessing upon him or her, we have succeeded in forgiving. But again, forgiveness is often a gradual process that may take months or years.

To finalize your act of forgiveness, you may find it helpful to write a statement of release to your ex. It could be sent or just written for your own benefit. The woman described earlier, who was struggling to forgive her ex, is a good example of what can happen in overcoming the hurt of the past. She said in her release statement:

Dear Jim,

I release you from the responsibility I gave you to determine how I have been feeling because of our breakup. I never did understand all that happened to make you the way you were, and I probably never will. It doesn't matter now. What matters is I release you from the bitterness and resentment I have held toward you over the past three years. I release you from my expectations of who and what you should have been. I forgive you.

Pray for the strength of Jesus Christ in your life as you release your past to him. Freeing your ex-partner by means of forgiveness gives you freedom as well. And in doing this you are able to experience the abundance that Jesus Christ has for you.

Forgiveness does not require you to strike up a friendship with your ex, nor does it require you even to share your forgiveness with the person. In fact, if you feel a compelling need to start a friendship with your ex or to tell him or her about your forgiveness, this is an indication that you are not yet fully over the breakup.

Friendship?

I'd like to address the whole issue of friendship following a breakup. If the breakup happened because of some outside factor such as a career change, it's easier to remain friends. If one individual had personal problems, such as severe depression or major family problems, which necessitated giving more time to one's own mental health or one's family, here too it is easier to remain friends. Why? The members of the broken relationship are less likely to blame the other for wrongdoing, and this seems to be a major factor in determining whether or not two people will be friends after a breakup. The higher the degree of blame, the less likely it is two people will be able to remain friends.

When beliefs, behaviors, attitudes, and fear of intimacy are involved, blame creeps in. Some former couples remain friends because of business or ministry, or because they are taking classes together in college or because of a mutual desire to help someone in need.

One question to consider is, Why should you remain friends? Consider these questions from Scott Nelson's *Lost Lovers, Found Friends:*

1. What would make you want to maintain a friendship after the breakup?
2. What aspects of your ex-partner or the relationship do you miss most?
3. What would you hope to get for yourself out of the new friendship?
4. What unfinished business remains between you and your ex-partner?
5. What do you need to learn from your ex-partner that will improve your chances for a better relationship next time?

6. What kind of relationship would you like to maintain with your ex-partner? What would you like to do together? Talk about? How much time would you want to spend together?[4]

Are there any guidelines for when it is best not to be friends? Scott Nelson says it is best to avoid a friendship with your ex under these circumstances:

when you have evidence that you or your ex-partner are avoiding the reality of the change in your relationship

when the friendship is an unhealthy block to your personal growth and development

when mental or physical abuse plays a part in the way you behave together

when the relationship hinders formation of new relationships

when your repeated efforts to be friendly toward each other end up in emotionally draining disappointment

when you are maintaining contact purely to save face or to sport an image

when you or your partner simply do not want to be friends[5]

Physical Reminders

What do you do with the gifts or special items you obtained together? Do you destroy them, give them back, refuse to give them back, look at and touch them as much as possible? Remember, these are links to your former partner. The memories associated with them may be filled with emotion. You may have mementos and reminders of your relationship all around you, and if so each of these could trigger sadness. Each time you see one, there's a possibility your heart will sink and the tears will begin.

For some it's helpful to avoid doing anything with these physical reminders except to place them somewhere out of sight. Once you put the items away, don't go back to them for several weeks. I've talked with people who would take a picture out every other day or so to see if it would make them sad. It did. And the hurt continued at an unnecessary level.

One man shared that he took every memento and picture he had of his ex, dumped it on her front doorstep, rang the bell, and left. I asked if doing this helped him and he replied, "Not really. I was hurt and angry. I wanted to show her I didn't need her or any memory of her. Well, I've still got the memories. I wish I'd kept all that stuff."

One writer mentioned a "griefcase." This is where you store any physical reminder of your ex until you are ready to say good-bye to it. As you find more things, place them in the box without looking at the others. By putting these away you're being proactive about your recovery.

When you feel stronger, set aside a time and take out each item. This is the day for you to grieve and cry over each item. This can be painful. About this experience one woman said, "It's as though I took out each item to stare it down. I actually said to several items, 'you're not going to control me or ruin my day again.'" Often people will pick a very special day for this event such as an anniversary, birthday, or just a day that was special for the two of you. Don't allow any interruptions: turn off the phone, cell phone, beeper, and hang a *do not disturb* sign on the door.

As you sift through the memorabilia, don't hold back the tears; let them come. Look at each letter and read it out loud. Look at each item and ask yourself, "What do I remember about this? What does each one represent?" If you have recordings or videos, listen to them or watch them. Look at and touch everything you've kept. I've known people who have gone so far as to make a special meal with the foods they and their ex especially enjoyed.

Keep doing this until you're drained and there are no more tears. In fact, keep crying until you think, "I'm tired of this. This is ridiculous."

Then say good-bye out loud to each item and each memory. You will have both positive and painful memories to face. For many, this is a one-time event. Yes, feelings of loss and sadness will still exist, but you'll feel as though you've turned a corner in your recovery path. If an item or song still overwhelms you, schedule a time to face this item a week or two later. You are taking charge of your life by scheduling this special time of healing. This may sound odd, but it isn't really. It's a lot like making a doctor's appointment to take care of a physical problem. This is every bit as important.[6]

One More Love Letter

It is common to write a love letter in the beginning of a relationship. It is uncommon, however, to write a letter to conclude a relationship, yet doing so can go a long way toward putting a failed relationship to rest. In such a letter the idea is to collect all your thoughts and feelings—anger, pleas, rationalizations, concerns, or apologies—and write them down. Don't mail it, of course. This project could continue for several days, or it could be a one-time occurrence. It includes setting to rest your unfulfilled dreams with this person as well as what this individual will be missing as a result of not having you in his or her life. This is a cleansing exercise, especially when you read the letter aloud to an empty chair, give all the contents to God in prayer, free yourself from the tyranny of these thoughts over you, and say your final good-bye.

Stages 5 and 6: Resolution and Rebuilding

In these stages, which are both part of the same transition, you resolve to live without your ex and rebuild your life anew. You're finally able to talk about the future with a sense of hope. You've completed your detachment from the other person, hopefully without any lingering fears.

In closing this chapter, let me recap the three possible outcomes of a breakup: a change for the better, a change for the worse, or a return to the previous level of living. At the outset of the breakup, it is almost impossible to conceive of things changing for the better, especially if you are the one who was rejected. In the latter stages of the crisis, you may be able to see glimmers of possibility for positive change. Your judgments and decisions during this turning point in your life will make the difference in the outcome.[7]

8

Charting Progress

A client of mine asked, "How do I know I'm getting over this breakup and recovering in the way I need to? It's been four months now and at times I feel different and other times I don't. What's normal or is there a normal?" Have you asked similar questions? We want to know *when* it will happen and *how* we will know. We want an accurate self-evaluation.

In this chapter we'll focus on some ways to tell how or whether you're progressing through recovery. Keep in mind these tools and indications for determining progress vary from person to person; the last thing you want to do is compare yourself with others.

When you find yourself thinking and talking less and less about the relationship, you're progressing. What percentage of your time do you feel at peace about your breakup, and what percentage of your time do you feel anxious about it? If you find times of balance between peace and anxiety, you're progressing. It's important that

8

you experience a balance in your memories as well, when you remember both the good as well as the problem times.

During the initial period after a breakup, concentration comes with great difficulty. So if your concentration is improving, that too is progress. Also, it's a good sign when you begin to be more patient with the rate of your recovery. Most people are too hard on themselves, berating themselves for taking "too long" in their estimation of making progress.

When you find yourself thinking and talking less and less about the relationship, you're progressing.

It may be time to check where you've been and where you are today. Following are some exercises designed to help you see how much you've progressed. On a scale from zero to ten, zero being your overall condition when you broke up and ten being your overall condition when you completely recover, evaluate where you were three months ago compared to where you are now by circling one of the numbers. If your breakup occurred less than three months ago, evaluate your overall condition at the point of breakup compared to how you're doing now.

Three months ago or when the breakup occurred:

0	1	2	3	4	5	6	7	8	9	10
The Loss										Recovery

Today:

0	1	2	3	4	5	6	7	8	9	10
The Loss										Recovery

Another sign of recovery is when your depression begins lifting and you start enjoying life a little. Depression still may come and go, but if it seems to have less of

112

a grip on you, recovery is on the horizon. How would you characterize your level of depression today? Which of the following statements comes closest to describing your depression level?

❏ Depression seems to cloud my whole life.

❏ I'm just beginning to face the cause of my anger and do something about it.

❏ I'm confronting my depression and beginning to break free.

❏ I'm moving out of my depression.

You're recovering when you begin to take the energy of your anger and use it to move forward. You're getting a handle on your anger when you realize its source is hurt and fear. Which of the following statements most accurately describes your level of anger?

❏ I've not felt any anger yet.

❏ I'm just beginning to understand the anger part of my recovery.

❏ I'm right in the middle of dealing with my anger.

❏ I've already processed my anger.

Sometimes anger is directed at different people to varying degrees. Indicate in the following table the degree to which you're angry with yourself, God, and your ex-partner.

Yourself
❏ A lot ❏ Some ❏ Comes and Goes ❏ Not Much

God
❏ A lot ❏ Some ❏ Comes and Goes ❏ Not Much

113

Your Ex
❏ A lot   ❏ Some   ❏ Comes and Goes   ❏ Not Much

Another sign of recovery has to do with ability to function. My friend Beverly shared with me a few months after her breakup, "I'm starting to be functional again. It's not a chore to do the necessities of life again. For a while it was so difficult to crank myself up to do even simple maintenance tasks. I can laugh again, I'm not paranoid about what I listen to on the radio or watch on TV. I used to be on edge and get upset. Not now. It seems like I took a vacation from enjoyment for a while.

"I actually enjoyed looking at flowers the other day and went into a florist shop and bought some . . . for me! I'm also working out again. I love to run and even though I got out of shape and I'm sore, I'm running again. And that's helping my appetite. Food tastes better than ever now."

Did you isolate yourself after the breakup? Many people do. They don't want to be around others. But when you begin to recover, other people move from being draining to being energizing. And that's as it should be. But it's a process and it probably won't happen as fast as you want.

Have you ever been in the hospital for an operation? If so, you know the procedure. After the operation is over, you're taken to a recovery room. You stay there for a few hours until the effects of the anesthetic begin to wear off. The term *recovery* is a bit misleading for this room. It certainly doesn't mean total recovery. It actually means helping you adjust to the effects of the operation so you are ready for the real recovery, which will take time.

Think of it like this:

Recovery from loss is like having to get off the main highway every so many miles because the direct route is under reconstruction. The road signs reroute you through little towns you hadn't expected to visit and over bumpy roads you hadn't wanted to bounce around on. You are basically traveling in the appropriate direction. On the map, however, the course you are following has the look of shark's teeth instead of a straight line. Although you are gradually getting there, you sometimes doubt that you will ever meet up with the finished highway.[1]

Recovery doesn't mean a once-and-for-all conclusion to your loss and grief. It is a twofold process involving a reduction and eventually the elimination of pain associated with the breakup as well as the renewal of your ability to function normally in your day-to-day life. But recovery includes something else too: change. Your loss changes you. As someone once asked in a counseling session, "If I can't be the way I was before this breakup, what is all this about recovery? What does it mean? How can you recover, yet not return to your old self?" The question is not so much how you can recover without going back to your old self. The question is whether you'll ever recover if you're focused on going back to who you were before the breakup. No, the solution is to move forward, to allow your breakup to shape you so that you are stronger and wiser for the experience.

I have a scar from a childhood operation. When I see it, I'm reminded of the operation. Breakups leave an internal scar and as with some physical scars, this breakup is in such a sensitive place that you're likely to feel a twinge of pain now and again. There's no predicting when these twinges will come. However, some recover completely so the former relationship is a distant memory.

Recovery includes reinvesting in life, looking for new relationships and new dreams. But you could very well feel uncomfortable with whatever is new; that's not

115

unusual. You may have questions and concerns because your previous experience didn't turn out the way you thought it would. If you begin to hope or trust again, it is possible you will experience another breakup.

Do you realize that you have a choice in your recovery? Most people don't have a choice in their loss, but everyone has a choice in their recovery. You have a choice about whether you will be affected positively or negatively by the breakup.

I've talked to people who choose to live in denial and move through life as though nothing happened. I have talked to people who are stuck in the early stages of their grief who choose to live a life of bitterness and blame. They hate members of the opposite sex. "They're all the same" is a common refrain. Some become so hardened and angry that it's difficult to be around them for an extended period of time. They're not pleasant. They've made a choice. They seem to forget that life is full of losses, and we have the choice to do something constructive or destructive with the losses that come our way.

Soon I'm going to offer you some more self-evaluation tests, but before I do I'd like to encourage you to go through these evaluations with someone who can assist you with an objective viewpoint. Sometimes another person is the difference between a distorted view of reality and a clear view of reality.

You can gain a sense of your progress by evaluating changes in yourself, in your relationship with the person you lost, and in your relationships with other people. As you take and review the following evaluations, the conclusions you reach may help you determine where you are in your recovery and how far you have to go. On a scale from zero to ten, zero meaning "I disagree entirely" and ten meaning "I totally agree," rate your level of agreement with each statement.

CHANGES IN MYSELF BECAUSE OF MY LOSS

I have returned to normal levels of functioning in most areas of my life.

0   1   2   3   4   5   6   7   8   9   10

My overall symptoms of grief have declined.

0   1   2   3   4   5   6   7   8   9   10

My feelings do not overwhelm me when I think about my loss or when someone else mentions it.

0   1   2   3   4   5   6   7   8   9   10

Most of the time I feel all right about myself.

0   1   2   3   4   5   6   7   8   9   10

I enjoy myself without feeling guilty.

0   1   2   3   4   5   6   7   8   9   10

My anger has diminished, and when it occurs, it is handled appropriately.

0   1   2   3   4   5   6   7   8   9   10

I don't avoid thinking about things that could be or are painful.

0   1   2   3   4   5   6   7   8   9   10

I have the ability to think positively.

0   1   2   3   4   5   6   7   8   9   10

My ex-partner does not dominate my thoughts or my life.

0   1   2   3   4   5   6   7   8   9   10

I can handle special days or dates without being totally overwhelmed by memories.

0   1   2   3   4   5   6   7   8   9   10

I can remember the loss on occasion without pain and without sadness.

0   1   2   3   4   5   6   7   8   9   10

117

I believe there is meaning and significance to my life.

0   1   2   3   4   5   6   7   8   9   10

I see hope and purpose in life, in spite of my loss.

0   1   2   3   4   5   6   7   8   9   10

I have energy and can feel relaxed during the day.

0   1   2   3   4   5   6   7   8   9   10

I no longer fight the fact that the loss has occurred. I have accepted it.

0   1   2   3   4   5   6   7   8   9   10

I am learning to be comfortable with who I am now as a single person.

0   1   2   3   4   5   6   7   8   9   10

I understand that my feelings over the loss will return periodically, and I can understand and accept that.

0   1   2   3   4   5   6   7   8   9   10

I understand what grief means and have a greater appreciation for it.

0   1   2   3   4   5   6   7   8   9   10

Changes in My Relationship with the Person I Lost

I remember our relationship realistically—with both positive and negative memories.

0   1   2   3   4   5   6   7   8   9   10

The relationship I have with the person I lost is appropriate.

0   1   2   3   4   5   6   7   8   9   10

I don't feel compelled to hang on to the pain.

0   1   2   3   4   5   6   7   8   9   10

118

My life has meaning even though this person is not a part of my life.

0   1   2   3   4   5   6   7   8   9   10

Changes I Have Made in Adjusting to My New World

I am open about my feelings in other relationships.

0   1   2   3   4   5   6   7   8   9   10

I feel it is all right for life to go on even though this person has left me.

0   1   2   3   4   5   6   7   8   9   10

I have developed an interest in people and things outside myself that have no relationship to the person I lost.

0   1   2   3   4   5   6   7   8   9   10

I have put the loss in perspective.

0   1   2   3   4   5   6   7   8   9   10

Are You Stuck?

Sometimes as you try to recover from a broken relationship, you end up getting stuck, like a car stalled on the side of the road. There are some warning signs, however, that will let you know whether you're stuck. One warning sign is an inability to accept what has happened. I've talked to some who just wouldn't accept what had happened. One woman said, "He was just upset. I know he didn't really mean it. He'll be calling soon." The pain of facing the loss is too much, so you hold on to a "togetherness fantasy."

Another warning sign is an isolation of oneself from others. This will happen to some degree even if you're not stuck, but it should not go on endlessly. For some, with-

119

drawal is selective. For others, it's total. If you withdraw for too long, the isolation begins to feed on itself and the grief will grow rather than decreasing.

Some people seem to stop living. They quit eating, quit going to work, quit doing all the things that people normally do. At first this may be expected but as an ongoing pattern it's a warning sign. June, a single mother of two, shared, "At first, my two children understood but after several months they'd had it. They told me I looked terrible and they were tired of making their own lunches. When they said they needed me to be their mom again, I heard them. In two weeks I buried my ex-partner emotionally, quit neglecting myself, and got back into life."

A very real problem for many is a dependence on alcohol or drugs.

A very real problem for many is a dependence on alcohol or drugs. It's a way to find short-lived relief and comfort, and when it's over the user does not go back to life as usual; he or she feels worse. I've known some who never used before the breakup and then plunged into substance abuse afterward. Drugs and alcohol do not solve grief; they prolong it.

If an individual thinks or talks obsessively about the breakup, he or she is probably stuck. If you've ever been around someone like this, it probably wasn't for long. Why? People like this demonstrate little progress in their recovery. They have a one-track mind, and others grow tired of hearing the same old song. The more a person thinks or talks about the loss, the more the pain is intensified. It's like hitting yourself again and again in the same place. There's constant damage. And there's little energy left for moving on.[2]

What can you do if you're having a difficult time moving forward? The following suggestions will help you take control of your situation.

1. *Try to identify what it is that doesn't make sense to you about your breakup.* Perhaps it is a vague question about God's purpose in this. Or it could be a specific question (e.g., "Why did this have to happen to me now, after all the time I invested?"). Ask yourself, "What is it that is bothering me the most?" Keep a card with you for several days to record your thoughts as they emerge.
2. *Identify the emotions you feel during each day.* Are you experiencing sadness, anger, regret, hurt, or guilt? What are the feelings directed at? Has the intensity of the feelings decreased or increased during the past few days? If your feelings are vague, identifying and labeling them will diminish their power over you.
3. *Identify the steps or actions you are taking to help you move ahead and overcome this breakup.* Identify what you have done in other relationships that helped you, or ask a trusted friend for help.
4. *Be sure you are sharing your loss and grief with others who can listen to you and support you during this time.* Don't look for advice givers but those who are empathetic and don't mind listening to what you have to say.
5. *Find a person who has experienced a similar loss.* It would be helpful to find or help organize a Relationship Recovery Group similar to a Divorce Recovery Group. Reading books or stories about those who have survived similar experiences can be helpful.
6. *Identify the positive characteristics and strengths of your life that have helped you before.* Which of these will help you at this time in your life?
7. *Spend time reading the Psalms.* Many of them reflect the struggle of human loss but give the comfort and assurance that are from God's mercies. See Psalms 34:6; 46:1; 138:3; and 147:3.

121

8. *When you pray, share your confusion, your feelings, and your hopes with God.* Be sure to be involved in the worship services of your church because worship is an important element in recovery and stabilization.
9. *Think about where you want to be in your life two years from now.* Write out some of your dreams and goals. Just setting some goals may encourage you to keep moving forward.
10. *Remember that understanding your grief intellectually is not sufficient.* It can't replace the emotional experience of living through this time. You need to be patient and allow your feelings to catch up with your mind. Expect mood swings, and remind yourself of these through notes placed in obvious places. Mood swings are normal.

Recovery is a back-and-forth process. One of the best ways to mark your progress is through a personal journal. This will give you proof that you are making progress even though your feelings say otherwise. Your journal is your own private property and is not for anyone else to read. It is an expression of what you are feeling and your recovery climb. It can be written in any style. It can be simple statements, poems, or prayers that reflect your journey. The authors of the *Grief Adjustment Guide* offer some helpful suggestions for a journal:

1. You may find it helpful to make time every day to write at least a short paragraph in your journal. At the end of a week, review what you have written to see small steps of progress toward grief recovery. Writing at least a line or two every day is the most effective way to keep a journal.

2. Some people write in their journals a few times each week, reviewing them at the end of the week and at the end of each month.

If you have trouble getting started, look over the following list of suggested beginnings from Dwight Carlson's *When Life Isn't Fair*. Find one that fits what you are feeling or need to express and use it to "jump start" your writing for the day:

1. My biggest struggle right now is . . .
2. The thing that really gets me down is . . .
3. The worst thing about my loss is . . .
4. When I feel lonely . . .
5. The thing I most fear is . . .
6. The most important thing I've learned is . . .
7. The thing that keeps me from moving on is . . .
8. I seem to cry most when . . .
9. I dreamed last night . . .
10. I heard a song that reminded me of . . .
11. A new person I've come to appreciate is . . .
12. I get angry when . . .
13. Part of the past that keeps haunting me is . . .
14. What I've learned from the past is . . .
15. Guilt feelings seem to come most when . . .
16. The experiences I miss the most are . . .
17. New experiences I enjoy the most are . . .
18. The changes I least and most like are . . .
19. My feelings sometimes confuse me because . . .
20. I smelled or saw something today that reminded me of . . .
21. A new hope I found today is . . .
22. New strengths I've developed since my loss are . . .
23. I feel close to God today because . . .
24. I am angry at God today because . . .
25. For me to find and have balance, I . . .

26. I got a call or letter from a friend today that . . .
27. My friend, _____, had a loss today, and I . . .[3]

If one of these doesn't fit, then write about what you *are* feeling. You could start with just one word (*misery, longing, hope,* or whatever), then describe that feeling with phrases or sentences. If you need to, cry as you write, but keep writing until there is nothing more to say about that feeling.

Your journal is yours to say and feel what is in your heart and mind. It is your way of crystallizing the feelings of loss. Dealing with your feelings one at a time in a written, tangible form is a good way to "own" your feelings and respond to them in an organized way. Grief often involves a tangle of feelings; writing them down is a great way to isolate and experience catharsis with each one.

Monitor what you write. When you begin to write more about what is happening *today* and less about the person you have lost, you'll know that healing and adjustment are indeed taking place. Though the process may seem painfully slow, look for signs of progress.[4]

Slippery Slope of Recovery

When an arm breaks, it's put into a cast—immobilized so that it does not sustain more damage before it heals. You need to do the same thing with your heart. In other words, beware of rebound relationships. Protect your heart. Put it in a cast until it can heal. Granted, this is hard to do. You have unmet needs—socially, physically, spiritually. You may feel as though there's a gaping hole in your gut, and you want to fill it *now*. With that kind of pressure, you can make awful decisions. You might think, "Who cares if this person shares my values, my interests, my faith? It's a warm body!"

124

Rebound relationships of any sort are more likely to hurt you than help you. Not only are such relationships shortsighted and based on desperation, they also set you up for additional injury.[5]

The authors of *Fresh Start* described what is needed in this way:

Fresh Start co-founder Bob Burns began using the term *slippery slope* in reference to an exercise played at Virginia Military Institute. Two teams of students would be put into a muddy pit. The goal: Get your whole team out and keep the other team in. Of course the whole business got pretty messy. Just when you thought you were safely out of the pit, some enemy would pull you back in.

And that's exactly how it works when you are getting over a relationship trauma. You think you're out of the pit, but your "enemies"—reminders, doubts, worries, or perhaps the people who put you down to begin with—keep dragging you down again. This is what the slippery slope looks like:

The Slippery Slope
Point of Trauma

Old Lifestyle	New Lifestyle
Denial	
Anger	Forgiveness
Bargaining	
Depression	Acceptance

While the slippery slope is common in all grieving situations, it is especially prevalent when a person rushes through the grief. When we hurry through the stages, it's likely that something will trip us up.

God does give us peace, but it usually comes at the end of a process that takes a couple of years. We can cite case after case of people who took their healing slowly, and

125

they have become much stronger, more mature believers. *This* is the best testimony to God's healing power.[6]

Perhaps you feel as though you're on that slope or you've been on it for a while. Most have. And you will slide back down the slope. Every slide is called a relapse. Relapses are normal, and as strange as this may seem, if you have relapses, it's an indication that you're recovering even if it doesn't feel like it. Here are some relapse triggers.

Relapses occur when you begin looking at how far you have to go to recover and you get overwhelmed.

Relapses occur when you feel you're different than others or should be and become overconfident.

Relapses occur when you see someone who reminds you of your former partner or when actually running into them.

When you fall down the slope the first time, it's hard to get back up. But it's easier after falling because you've been there and know how to climb out.

What triggers you to slide down the slope? If you can identify what it is, you may be able to anticipate and even prevent a few slides. If not, you may at least be aware of what's coming.[7]

Hopefully you are at a place in your recovery where you can complete what I refer to as a "relationship debriefing." By completing this, you will learn even more about yourself and future relationships. Feel free either to write your answers in the book or to use a journal.

1. What were your initial thoughts and responses to your ex when you first met?

2. What do you think this person's initial reaction to you was like? What did he or she think? Did the two of you ever discuss your initial reactions?
3. If you weren't that interested at first, what brought about the change? Has this been a pattern in your relationship?
4. At the beginning who did the pursuing? Did this pattern continue throughout the relationship?
5. Were both you and your partner available for a permanent relationship?
6. Throughout a relationship feelings can change and fluctuate. What were your changes on the following scales? Circle a number.

Beginning of the relationship:

0	1	2	3	4	5	6	7	8	9	10
Negative		Neutral		Average			Very Positive			Love

Middle of the relationship:

0	1	2	3	4	5	6	7	8	9	10
Negative		Neutral		Average			Very Positive			Love

End of the relationship:

0	1	2	3	4	5	6	7	8	9	10
Negative		Neutral		Average			Very Positive			Love

When the relationship was over:

0	1	2	3	4	5	6	7	8	9	10
Negative		Neutral		Average			Very Positive			Love

7. If feelings changed at times, what was the cause?
8. How would you chart your ex's feelings for you at the various stages? Use the scales above, but draw a box to indicate your ex-partner's level of affection.
9. When the relationship started, did you have any reservations? If so, what were they? Did your friends have

any reservations? If so, what were they? Did your family have any reservations? If so, what were they?

10. What do you wish you knew about this person at the beginning of the relationship that you do know now?
11. How would this have made a difference?
12. What didn't your ex-partner know about you at the beginning of the relationship that could have made a difference?
13. What do you wish you would have done differently?
14. In what way did you discuss problems in the relationship?
15. Who brought up the problems? Who was most resistant? Did the discussions bring about positive changes?
16. How did the relationship end? Who brought it up first? Who resisted and how?
17. What might have made this relationship work?
18. What are your thoughts and feelings about your ex at this time?
19. What specifically did you learn from this experience that will help you in the future?
20. What are some reasons that your breakup was ultimately for the best?[8]

Part 3

Moving On

9

Successfully Single

Listen to the words of a twenty-four-year-old client of mine: "It's hard to be alone again. It's been two years since I've been single. I guess you hope that each relationship will turn into a lasting one, but over the years it hasn't been that way. Oh, there are times when I've been contented with being alone, but not this time. I feel lonely and it hurts."

Loneliness—a feeling with many dimensions. It's the feeling that you don't matter, that you've been cut off from others. Loneliness is when you feel isolated, deserted, or even banished from relationships with others. It's the feeling that even though you're in a room full of people, you're still all alone. The word itself has a mournful and eerie sound. It is cold like the earth in winter when the birds and flowers have abandoned it.

A songwriter described loneliness like this:

> If I were a cloud, I'd sit and cry,
> If I were the sun, I'd sit and sigh,
> But I'm not a cloud, nor am I the sun,
> I'm just sitting here, being no one.
>
> If I were the wind, I'd blow here and there,
> If I were the rain, I'd fall everywhere,
> But I'm not the wind, nor am I the rain,
> I'm just no one—feeling pain.
>
> If I were the snow, I'd fall oh so gently,
> If I were the sea, waves would roll o'er me,
> But I'm not the snow, nor am I the sea,
> I'm just no one—and lonely.[1]

The clue to what loneliness is really like can be found in the line from Psalm 142:4: "No one cares about me" (ICB).

In their separation from God, Adam and Eve were the first to experience loneliness.

Jesus felt the pangs of loneliness. He was misunderstood by many and only partially understood by his disciples. He suffered loneliness in the Garden of Gethsemane, in Pilate's judgment hall, and on the cross (see Matt. 26–27). Jesus' heart was full of love for his people, so it's no wonder he felt loneliness. His love was rejected.

Perhaps the words of David are your words: "[Lord,] turn to me and be gracious to me, for I am lonely and afflicted" (Ps. 25:16 AMP).

It's normal to feel lonely now and then. That's not the problem. The problem is when we feel lonely constantly, and I've seen this in some of the most gregarious men and women you could ever meet.

Loneliness arises when the relationship you once had becomes the central focus of your life. Life revolves around one person, who is no longer present. It seems as though there's nothing left to hang on to. And if your partner is the one who called it quits, you have the additional pain of rejection.

Loneliness can lead to a state of being frozen—you want love but the fear of reaching out to accept the love that friends might offer can limit you from supportive relationships. Loneliness arises when your focus is on what you lost, and you forget about friends or the potential for friends.

Loneliness is a season that you'll go through as someone who is newly single again, but remember what a season is like. It is short. It doesn't last forever. Loneliness is a part of grief, so as you grieve the feeling of loneliness will lift even without a significant person in your life.

Loneliness is a regular part of life when you have relationships. To be completely free from the risk of loneliness, a person would have to lead a life in which no one he ever cared about was lost or absent.

The feeling of loneliness is like the feeling of depression. It's not the problem. It alerts you to a problem. It's telling you something is wrong, and you need to discover what's wrong and take the appropriate steps to fix it. It's uncomfortable, but it prompts you to take action. If we give into loneliness and let it take up residence in our lives, we suffer endlessly. If instead we play host to loneliness as a temporary visitor whom we encourage to be on its way, then we move on in life.

Listen to the wise words of John Ortberg, who addressed the difficulty of loneliness and waiting in his book *If You Want to Walk on Water, You Have to Get out of the Boat*:

> Waiting on the Lord is a confident, disciplined, expectant, active and sometimes painful clinging to God.

Waiting on the Lord is the continual, daily decision to say, "I will trust you, and I will obey you. Even though the circumstances of my life are not turning out the way I want them to, and may never turn out the way I would choose, I am betting everything on you. I have no plan B."

Maybe you are single. As Americans, we live in a society where so often the assumption is that marriage is normal and being single is not. You feel the pain of that stigma.

Maybe you feel a legitimate longing for intimacy.

Maybe you feel a kind of loneliness that only God can heal, that another human being cannot rescue you from.

Waiting is so hard.

Maybe there is a potential relationship right at your fingertips, but you know it would not be honoring to God. Maybe you know in your heart it is not really the right person because that person does not share your ultimate commitment to God. Maybe that person is putting pressure on you to be involved sexually even though you are not married.

You are tempted to think, "I have been waiting long enough. I'm tired of waiting. I'm going to reach out for whatever satisfaction I can in this life and worry about the consequences later."

Will you wait on the Lord? Will you courageously say, "Okay, God. I will not get hooked up with a relationship that I know would dishonor you and bring damage to the souls of those involved. I will seek to build the best life that I can right where I am, not knowing what tomorrow holds. Even though I sometimes feel no one else understands how painful it is, I will trust you. I will wait."[2]

You Have a Choice

The first thing to realize is that you have a choice between "sad passivity " or "active solitude." The first consists of doing nothing, wandering through an apartment aimlessly, sleeping, drinking, overeating, taking tranquilizers, watching TV, or using drugs. This leads to a downward spiral from emotional and social isolation to depression. But in "active solitude" you engage in constructive activities such as exercise, painting, reading, taking a class on the Internet, or helping and serving others.[3] It's your choice.

Be selective in your friendships and relationships. If you're lonely, admit it. But before searching for people to fill the need, consider this: what would you do if you were isolated on an island for years like Tom Hanks in *Cast Away*? How would you fill your life? If you have a personal relationship with Jesus Christ, make the most of it. Talk with him. Read his Word. Spend time in fellowship with healthy Christians. Look for ways to serve God in ministry.

The first thing to realize is that you have a choice between "sad passivity" or "active solitude."

When self-pity hits, set a time limit on how long you allow yourself to wallow. It could be fifteen minutes, a half hour, or whatever. But after the time limit, focus on life and others and what you *do* have. Make a list of your blessings.

Do you have a close friend who can be a prayer partner? This is the kind of person who is like-minded and can hold you accountable to the Lord.

Too many who are in between relationships have said they need to be in a relationship or married in order to be happy or fulfilled. But this sounds more like dependency than anything else. Henry Cloud and John Townsend said, "If you are afraid of aloneness and abandonment, you cannot use the love of people who are truly there until you deal with your own fears. So, aloneness must be cured first."[4] Many believe, "When I am accepted by another, I will be satisfied and my life will be fulfilled." But no experience of approval leads to permanent satisfaction.

For those who are addicted to the approval and acceptance of another person, there is a high price to pay. The price tag includes an extreme vulnerability to the whims and subjective opinions of the people around you. Others can take advantage of your vulnerability and mistreat you, which leads to rejection. When we seek to fulfill our lives by depending on other people's perceptions of ourselves, we shut off God's blessing and his affirmation in our daily experience.

Pursue God

Years ago I heard an older counselor say, "You can't be happily married to another person unless you're happily married to yourself." It made sense. If I don't feel satisfied with who I am, another person isn't going to solve that. My relationship with God will. He's the one who brings wholeness and satisfaction.

Again, Cloud and Townsend: "Have a full life of spiritual growth, personal growth, vocational growth, altruistic service, hobbies, intellectual growth, and the like. The active growing life does not have the time or inclination to be dependent on a date. The more you have a full life of relationship with God, service to others, and interesting stimulating activities, the less you will feel like you need a relationship in order to be whole."[5]

Pursue wholeness. In addition to an active life, work on the issues that are in your soul. Whatever those issues are (past childhood hurts; destructive patterns in your relationships and work life; areas of brokenness, pain, and dysfunction), as you are resolving them your aloneness will be cured as well. It is a curious thing, but the process of spiritual growth itself can help cure aloneness.

As you grow spiritually, you will naturally grow closer to others and gain a fuller life.

Henry Cloud and John Townsend say, "The best boundary against giving in to bad relationships is your own willingness to do without such relationships. And this willingness comes from being grounded in God, having a support system, working out your issues, having a full life, and pursuing wholeness."[6] Some individuals make the pursuit of a marriage partner their life goal. But the pursuit of a relationship with God is much more fulfilling. Listen to the psalmist: "I sought the LORD, and he answered me; he delivered me from all my fears" (Ps. 34:4). When you pursue God, the pain of not having your ex-partner in your life diminishes. I've seen God take away not only the *pain* of a broken relationship but also the *fear* of never finding a marriage partner.

Dick Purnell, who was single until he was forty-two, said, "God's viewpoint is to pursue love, not marriage. He has given you your single years so you will learn how to love faithfully, to learn how to give yourselves to someone else in friendship, to learn how to become the right person, to learn how to walk with the Lord, to learn how to be sensitive to another person's needs, to learn how the opposite sex thinks and feels and to learn how to communicate your heart to others."[7]

Singles tell me they are looking for a mate who can really help them walk with God. But if you need someone else to help you know God intimately, you have problems. Your walk with God is supposed to be an independent personal relationship with him. It is not to be a vicarious, secondhand relationship through a mate or friend. Someone of the opposite sex who meets your specifications for godliness is not going to want you if you are a spiritual sponge. Each of us is responsible for our own walk with the Lord.

Instead of looking for the right person, singles should focus on becoming the right person. If you seek to be the right person, God will take care of finding the right mate for you according to his purpose for your life.[8] Have you ever considered that God can give you a quality of life right now that is better than anything you could ever create on your own? It's worth considering. Have you ever thanked God for where you are in your life right now? Perhaps you're not ready yet. You may be in too much pain. But that's the way to relieve the pain. Begin this process and you may be amazed at the results.

Singleness Is Not a Disease

When a number of people were asked what they thought of being single, the answers varied:

"Yeah, I guess it's all right, but just for a while. I wasn't made to be single."

"I can handle it. After all, it's been my life for thirty years."

"I can live as a single or in a relationship. But someday marriage has got to be there, I hope."

"I don't think I qualify for the gift of celibacy, so I've got to marry."

"Are you asking if I can be single for a while? Sure. Forever? I don't know."

What about you? What if it's your calling to be single the rest of your life? I know, some of you don't even want me to go there!

Unfortunately, too many single people believe life begins when they start a relationship. Some don't think it starts until marriage happens. Too many think their lives are in a holding pattern while they're single. The word "incomplete" comes to mind. Such singles are forever "future oriented" and are never satisfied with the present and all it has to offer.

Consider what Tim Stafford, senior writer for *Christianity Today*, has said about singleness: "God may want you to be single. He wants everyone to be single for at least a part of their life. And the Bible doesn't talk about singleness as being second rate. In fact, the Bible speaks positively about it."

In the Middle Ages, Christians went too far, and *marriage* was regarded as second rate. In recent times we seem to have swung the other way. Balance is the key. Both marriage and singleness are gifts from God.

Ponder for a moment the following facts about our Lord: Jesus Christ never married. He never had sexual intercourse. Yet he was perfect, and perfectly fulfilled. He lived the kind of life we want to imitate. That doesn't mean we should all be single; undoubtedly marriage is the best way for most men and women. But singleness need not be unhappy.

Paul wasn't married either, at least not at the height of his career. He addressed the single life in 1 Corinthians 7, calling it a gift. And Jesus himself, in Matthew 19:10–12, talks positively about the reasons some people should remain unmarried.

It saddens me to see single people who live life as though waiting for something else to happen. They act as though they are in limbo, waiting to become capable of life when that magic day at the altar finally arrives.

Of course, singles who live in this constant state of disappointment often become such poor specimens of humanity that no one wants to marry them anyway. More often they do get married, only to discover that a spouse is not the key to life; the initiative and character they should have developed before marriage is exactly what they lack

139

to make the most of marriage. And they are still lonely and frustrated.

Tim Stafford points out, "Our culture, especially Christian culture, has stressed repeatedly that a good marriage takes work. It venerates those who have been married for long periods of time. But I've seldom heard anyone emphasize the fact that a good single life also takes work. I've never heard anyone compliment a single for having created a good lifestyle. In our culture, telling single people they have received a gift is rather like convincing a small child that liver ought to taste good because it's 'good for you.' But singleness, as I see it, is not so much a burden as it is a set of opportunities."[9]

How to Determine If Singleness Is for You

Recognize that you are likely to be single only for a period of time (for example, until you are thirty) rather than for all of your life. Accept this season of your life. Don't fight it. Remember, it is easier to make a hasty decision for marriage than to reverse that decision once you are married. Here are some questions worth considering.

Are you able to live with the idea that you might remain single all your life?

Is your desire to serve God complicated by the thought of a marriage partner?

Are you able to enjoy yourself without feeling the need for a lot of dates?

Could you make a vow to God to remain single for a period of time?

Do you see the advantages of singleness outweighing the advantages of marriage? Have you ever made a list and compared?

Do you see God calling you to a form of service that would be difficult if you were married (for example, work in the inner city, work in primitive mission projects)?

Are you willing to accept or work toward accepting being single if this is what God wants?

A good way to determine whether God wants you to be single is to try it for a specific period of time. For example, you might go for one year without a date, devoting your normal dating time to serving others and God. If you fail, don't think you've fallen out of favor with God. This is just an experiment. It's similar to trying to go to the mission field; you may discover it's not for you. You can still serve God effectively wherever you are. However, you should be as open to God's call to single living as you are to any other call he might have for you.

What if God were to send you a letter that said something like this: "Not until you are satisfied, fulfilled, and content with being loved by me alone, with giving yourself totally and unreservedly to me, with having an intensely personal and unique relationship with me, will you be capable of having the perfect human relationship that I have planned for you. You will never be united with another until you are united with me—exclusive of anyone or anything else, exclusive of any other desires or longings.

"I want you to stop planning, stop wishing, and allow me to give you the most thrilling plan existing—one that you cannot imagine. I want you to have the best. Please allow me to bring it to you. You just keep watching me, expecting the best. Keep listening and learning the things that I tell you. You just wait, that's all. Don't be anxious. Don't worry.

"Don't look around at the things others have received. Don't look around at the things you think you want. Keep

141

looking at me, or you will miss what I want to show you. And then, when you are ready, I'll surprise you with a love far more wonderful than any you've dreamed of. You see, until you are ready, and until the one I have for you is ready (I am working even at this moment to have both of you ready at the same time), until you are both satisfied exclusively with me, you won't be able to experience the love that exemplifies your relationship with me.

"Dear one, I want you to have this most wonderful love. I want you to see in the flesh a picture of your relationship with me, and to enjoy materially and concretely the everlasting union of beauty, perfection, and love. What I offer you is myself. Know that I love you utterly. I am God. Believe it and be satisfied."

Fireproof Reentry

Help for Those Who Are Dating Again

The thought of dating again can be exciting—and scary. One minute you're daydreaming about Mr. or Ms. Right, the next minute you see and hear a nose-diving airplane descending through the clouds to its fiery demise. This combination of fantasy and fear affects many as they contemplate the brave step of reentering the dating world.

Your first few dates may not be the best experiences. You might be on edge and feel awkward. You might be expecting the worst or on your guard too much. The signals you're likely to give off will be a mixture of curiosity and reluctance: "I'm interested, but keep away." Your emotional wounds may still be wounds that haven't yet turned to scars. Don't worry. All of this is normal, so don't give up. The purpose of this chapter is to help you start dating again by giving you a number of tips to keep in mind.

Be Cautious

For a number of years the action-packed police television show *Hill Street Blues* captivated viewers. The offices at this precinct were occupied by a motley group of characters. In fact, as a viewer you weren't sure if you'd even want their help! Each day a morning briefing took place. It was often chaotic and disruptive. But just before dismissing the rowdy officers, the sergeant would pause and say, "Let's be careful out there!" He was warning them to be alert, to keep their guard up, and to avoid slacking off because the unpredictable could and would happen.

Scripture warns again and again to "be on your guard." Listen to these warnings: "Only be careful, and watch yourselves" (Deut. 4:9); "Be careful to do what the LORD your God has commanded you" (Deut. 5:32); "Be careful to obey all that is written in the Book" (Josh. 23:6); "Be careful to do what is right" (1 Cor. 10:12); "Be careful, then, how you live" (Eph. 5:15); and "Be careful that none of you be found to have fallen short" (Heb. 4:1).

Be on your guard, Jesus said, against hypocrisy (see Matt. 16:6–12); against greed (see Luke 12:15); against persecution from others (see Matt. 10:17); against false teaching (see Mark 13:22–23); and, above all, against being unready for the Lord's return (see Mark 13:32–37). "Be careful," Jesus said in Luke 21:34, "or your hearts will be weighed down with dissipation, drunkenness and the anxieties of life." Being careful means to be wary, to keep your eyes open, to be alert. Let your guard down just once, and you may do something that will cause great harm.[1]

Don't Date Someone You Don't Know

The best romantic relationships grow out of friendships. It's also much easier to relax and be yourself in the beginning of a dating relationship if the person you date is already a friend.

The Grand Canyon, as awe inspiring as it is today, didn't begin so grandly. The first trickle of the Colorado River gave no hint as to what it would carve out in time. Today's Grand Canyon tourists can hike or take a mule-train ride to the bottom of the canyon, in places more than a mile below the canyon's rim. The width of the canyon today ranges from four to eighteen miles, and the length from its beginnings in the Little Colorado River to Lake Meade is 217 miles.

Lifelong romantic love, like the Grand Canyon, usually develops from small beginnings. Now, not all rivers create the Grand Canyon, and not all opposite-sex friendships end in the lifelong love of marriage. But the latter does happen, and thankfully it happens far more often than rivers create canyons![2]

Realize What You Can and Can't Control

I've heard both men and women say some variation of the following: "One of the things that holds me back from entering a new relationship is the fact that I can't control the outcome." That's true. You can't control what's going to happen, nor can you control the other person's feelings toward you. So, my advice is to give yourself permission to be without control in those areas. What you can control is your own responses to the other person, so make sure your responses are in line with your feelings. Don't send mixed signals. Don't move too quickly. Be cautious, with both your own heart and that of whom you're dating.

Identify Your Fears

How has fear played a part in your relationships? Have you ever been in a relationship in which you wanted to connect with the other person but you were afraid to move ahead? Or perhaps it was your partner who wanted to reach out to you but was immobilized by fear. Here are some examples of common fears:

Be cautious, with both your own heart and that of whom you're dating.

"If I continue in this relationship, I'll end up fulfilling needs in his life, but I'm not so sure my own needs will be met."

"If I continue in this relationship, I may have to forego my independence in order to be close. I'm not sure I want to make that trade-off."

"If I continue in this relationship, I'll have to reveal more and more of who I am, which will increase the pain if in the end I get rejected."

"If I continue in this relationship, I could get attached. If my partner decides to leave me, the hurt will be too much to bear."

"If I continue in this relationship, I could end up being dominated and controlled."

"If I continue in this relationship, I'm not sure I can be who I am without scaring off my partner."

"If I continue in this relationship, my partner might become too dependent on me. I don't want to feel suffocated."

"If I continue in this relationship, I will have to give up even more of my single lifestyle and there are certain aspects of it I don't want to let go."

"If I continue in this relationship, I'm concerned about how the children will react."

"If I continue in this relationship, my partner may turn into an entirely different person."

"If I continue in this relationship, I may miss opportunities with other people."[3]

Have you ever experienced any of these fears? If so, you're not alone. The important thing is to identify which fears affect you, so you are aware of them. Once you've identified them, then you can evaluate whether your fears are valid.

Don't Fall for Myths

I've seen many singles cripple their relationship's potential by believing myths. These are inaccurate beliefs that come from the negative experiences of a small number of people that then are generalized as gospel truth.

Has anyone ever told you there aren't enough eligible partners out there? This is a myth that often makes the rounds in Christian singles groups. I can see why because in the majority of Christian singles groups there are usually three or four women to every man. You might have to be creative as you look for a potential partner, but that doesn't mean there's a shortage of potential partners. In fact, if you're willing to be creative in your search and go beyond your immediate social circles, there's no end to the list of eligible singles.

Another relationship myth is summed up by this statement: "I'll never find the kind of person I really want, so why bother?" One of my closest friends was quite selective

147

in his search for the love of his life. You can read about his criteria on pages 120–125 of my book *Finding Your Perfect Mate*. After this book was published women wrote to me to find out whether this man actually existed or if I made him up. He really does exist, and after dating numerous women over a period of several years my friend did find the ideal person for him. He didn't discover her in the way he thought he would. He never thought he would marry a woman with children, as he was in his fifties and never had any children before. But it's amazing how God works. His wife has three children from a prior marriage, and he loves being a stepdad. One day he told me, "Norm, I had to wait until I was in my fifties to find the woman of my dreams. And I did. I'm so glad I waited."

Another myth is: "I'm too old to start looking, let alone dating." Who put time limits on looking and dating? Only you can do that. I regularly encourage singles in their sixties, seventies, and eighties to keep on dating.

One more myth is related to the loser mentality: "I'm a loser and that's all I'll ever find," or "All the good ones are taken." An important thing to remember when dating is that you will meet some people who are more compatible with you than others, but you will never find a perfect person. The only place perfect people exist is in our minds.[4]

Beware of Rebounding

If you've ever played basketball, you know how helpful it is to have players on your team who excel at "rebounding"—players who can leap up and grab missed shots so your team gains or keeps possession of the ball. Relational rebounding is a different story.

Relational rebounding is when a person goes immediately from one relationship to another without taking time to heal from the end of the first. Often the rebounder is in intense pain and instead of experiencing the loss and grief on his own, he tries to cover some of the pain by entering a new relationship. The feelings associated with the new relationship are much more positive than the pain of the last one. In a sense, the new partner is being used as an anesthetic to numb some of the hurt.

If you enter a new relationship with a load of pain, your hurt is likely to distort your perception of the other person, and it will be difficult in this state to make an emotional connection. Rebounding hinders the rebounder from healing and contaminates a new relationship. Both people need to be stable and healthy for a relationship to have a chance.

One woman described the process of rebounding in my counseling office: "I feel as though I'm on a merry-go-round, bumper car, and roller coaster all at the same time. I have to be on the go constantly or I think I'll go bananas. I'm always doing something and jumping into one relationship after another—and unfortunately, one bed after another. I don't like myself for doing this, and it makes me feel even worse about the relationship I lost. I've decided to find some more constructive things to do with my time and to stay home on Thursday and Friday night each week to prove that I'm able to do it. It hurts, but I think I'll recover by doing this, and I'm sure I can grow through this experience. I don't want to be chained to him forever, and I think I have been."

Some may be ready for a relationship earlier than others, but you need to ask this question: "Am I being considered for who I am, a unique person whom this other person is interested in pursuing, or is this person expecting me to be a cure?" The other question is: "Am I looking at the person I'm interested in as a cure, or am I attracted to her for who she is?"

How can you tell for sure whether this new person in your life is a rebounder? First of all, before you invest a lot

149

of time in the new relationship, the two of you should discuss your last relationships. If either was long-term, go into detail about the type of relationship it was, what caused the termination, how long ago it took place, what you've done to recover, and how you're doing in your adjustment. This isn't being intrusive, but safe and practical.

You may want to look for clues to how similar or dissimilar you are to his or her former partner. I have seen many people choose men or women who are just like their former partners, defects and all. These replacements will probably be just as disappointing as the previous partners were. But something drives some individuals to prove they can have relationships with a particular kind of person. This is why many daughters who have distant fathers choose husbands who are very much like their fathers.

Before any person can move ahead with a new relationship, it's necessary to say good-bye to the former relationship. It's the final step of grieving over a relationship.

I can't make this next statement strong enough. **Do not become involved or even look for another relationship until you have fully worked through the results of the last broken relationship.** If you don't, the hurt and damage from the last relationship will contaminate the next one. Whatever is unfinished about the last relationship comes with you as baggage. Many bring the residue of more than one broken relationship into the next one.

The author of *Dating Secrets of the Ten Commandments* says, "Some people date and break up so frequently that they become hardened; they don't realize the harmful effect having their heart broken has on them. They pick up the pieces and glue them back together so they can go straight into the next relationship. But the cracks are still there and they are all too obvious. It is hardly fair of such people to expect dating to go as well as it should."[5]

Rebounders tend to manifest certain characteristics. If the person you're dating makes unreasonable requests of you, be cautious. This could be a rebound symptom or the result of deeply ingrained personality traits. In either case, it's not healthy for you. Often the rebounder still has a lot of anger for his or her former partner. This anger could lead to resentment, which can create a bitterness not just toward the original source, but perhaps to other people—even you. You may want to discover whether your current partner has a pattern of blaming others for misfortune. You certainly don't want to be an addition to his or her trophy case of "bad guys."

Stay Away from Prebounders

There is a second kind of person who is hazardous to relational health. One author called this kind of person a *prebounder*. Prebounders are very similar to rebounders except they are still involved in one relationship while looking for a new one. Prebounders are looking for a safety net to fall into once the current relationship fails. Prebounding is deceptive, not to mention a violation of trust in the current relationship.

Sometimes the prebounder "falls in love" with another and then tries to figure out what to do with his or her current partner. But who's to say he or she won't keep two relationships going at once? I've seen individuals have as many as five relationships at one time. If you find yourself in a relationship with a prebounder, get out as soon as possible.

To follow are some questions to discuss with your new love interest that will help you detect either rebounding or prebounding. A generous way to proceed is to start by giving your own honest answers to the questions and then to pose them to your dating partner.

1. How frequently do you think about your former partner and in what way? Is it negative or positive?

151

2. How frequently do you have contact with your former partner and in what way? What is the purpose? What feelings do you experience on these occasions?

3. In what ways do you think your current partner is similar to this former partner?

4. On a scale from 1 to 10, 1 being "not worried at all" and 10 being "extremely afraid," to what extent do you have a fear that this past relationship may repeat itself again?

5. On a scale from 1 to 10, 1 being "none at all" and 10 being "all the time," to what extent do you experience guilt over the previous relationship? How might this guilt affect your ability to build a relationship with another individual?

6. On a scale from 1 to 10, 1 being "none at all" and 10 being "extremely angry," to what extent do you harbor anger about the previous relationship? If there is anger, what can be done to resolve it?

I realize you may be thinking, "My current partner and I could never discuss these issues." But in time you should. If you're *never* able to discuss them, what does this tell you about your relationship? If you are involved with a rebounder or prebounder, you're being used as a crutch. And when a broken leg heals, the crutch is discarded.[6]

Think of it this way. If you go to a new medical doctor, how does he help you? First, he takes a medical history by asking some questions that don't always seem to pertain to the ailment you brought to his attention. But in order to evaluate you properly, the doctor needs the total picture. Similarly, it's important to learn about the history of your dating partner, so you'll have an idea of his or her background. This information will help you to spot potential trouble areas, like rebounding or prebounding, but it will also help you get to know your partner better.

Bad Candidates

Sometimes courtship problems arise because one becomes involved with an individual who is just not a good candidate from the outset. Some relationships have such barriers to begin with; they will never survive. Neil Clark Warren's book *How to Tell in Two Dates or Less* . . . has some merit, if one is willing to apply what he says. Some people are drawn to others who are so different in numerous ways that you know right away it would never work. My counselee Tom shared, "One day after my sixth relationship in two years failed, it dawned on me. Maybe I'm drawn to women with whom I know it won't work out because it's safe. I won't have to deal with a commitment."

One of the interesting factors I've come across in years of counseling singles is how often a person will be drawn to a person who is unavailable in one way or another. Sometimes the person is already involved with another individual. Some are geographically unavailable. For some it's romantic when he or she lives in Oregon and his or her partner lives in Texas. Such couples may see each other once or twice a year. Some say this is no longer the problem it used to be thanks to phones, visual phones, e-mail, and so forth, but nothing replaces being with one another. I've seen too many courtships carried on by e-mail whereby individuals ended up marrying strangers.

I talked with Rachel who said, "Commitment for me hasn't been easy, especially after I've been hurt so much. My girlfriends warned me about Al. Two of them dated him and he couldn't commit. Maybe I thought it was my girlfriends' problem and not Al's. You know, he'd find me irresistible and we'd get married and live happily ever after, but it didn't work that way. I don't think he's marriage material at all. I could have avoided all this pain and grief if I hadn't deluded myself."[7]

Questions to Ask before Entering a New Relationship

Following is a list of questions to consider before entering a new relationship. I've phrased them using the first-person pronouns "I," "me," and "my" to help make the questions more personal.

Over the years how satisfying have my relationships been? What descriptive adjectives would I use to describe them? If my relationships have not been satisfying, what was my own contribution to the problems that developed? What criteria have I used to select new partners in the past? Was this good criteria?

What do I hope to gain from a long-term relationship? What is my end goal? What do I have to contribute?

How do I feel about myself as a person? Am I hoping to find someone who is stronger, wealthier, better looking, more ambitious, more intelligent, or more educated than I? If so, why? Am I hoping to find something in this other person that I can't find in myself? Am I hoping to share in someone else's dream, rather than my own?

How strong is my identity? Is it flexible or frozen in concrete?

Do I take risks? If so, do I get involved in unhealthy risks? Do I thrive on the excitement of the unknown, or does that scare me? What's the biggest risk I've taken in a relationship and what was the purpose? What did I learn?

Do I accept the fact that I can't change anyone else? To what degree do I feel threatened when the other person is different from how I would like him or her to be? Would I be more comfortable in a relationship with my clone or a total opposite?

Do I do anything that prevents me from getting what I want in a relationship? Is there anything I'm afraid of or avoiding?

Am I still attached to a former partner in a way that keeps me from moving on and building a new relationship? Do I have any unresolved grief or unfinished business with a former partner? What do my past partners have in common? Was there information about my partners that I chose to ignore at the beginning of each relationship? If so, why?

Do I have any unfinished business with either of my parents that might keep me from relating to a partner? If so, what do I want to do about this?

How much do I feel a need to control others, the events in my life, and my environment? What would my friends say about this? How does a need for control create problems for me? For others?

Am I serious about developing a committed relationship or do I just want to date? What is the evidence of this?

Do I tend to look to others for my sense of worth in a dating relationship? How much power do I give to a dating partner to make or break my day? To what degree do I need the attention and approval of this person? Does this create a problem for me or others, and if so, how?

To what degree has my life revolved around dating partners?

What do I feel shameful about? What do I feel guilty about? What would it take for me to forgive myself?

Do I have any behaviors that seem to be out of my control? What would others say? How do these create a problem for me? If so, do I want to change?

How do I get my way? What kind of power do I use: direct, assertive power, or indirect (aggressive, passive, manipulative) power? Or do I see myself as having little or no power in my life? What's the evidence to support this?

What are the reasons another person would be interested in me?

How intelligent does my significant other have to be? Is this a reasonable expectation?[8]

These questions are designed to help you think through issues that are important to the health of future relationships. Mulling them over and talking about them with friends will put you in a better position to reenter the dating world. You might also find the questions in the appendix helpful.

11

Avoiding Problems Before They Happen

Men and woman have asked, "What's the best way to select a potential partner?" One of the best ideas I found came from another writer. Go to the supermarket and spend an hour in the produce section. Watch the shoppers select fruits and vegetables. Do they just grab items randomly? Not usually. They examine the fruit. It may be a banana. People don't want it too ripe or too green. They don't want it bruised. They compare one bunch with another to make sure they've selected the right one. If people spend this much time picking out a banana, doesn't it make sense that they should spend a good deal more time picking out a lifelong companion?

Before you consider moving into a long-term relationship and possibly marriage, let's consider some "I don't need this" kind of problems. If these problems exist, it's time to consider stopping the relationship before it gets started.

Commitmentphobia

In the last two decades the English language has been inundated with new words that attempt to label relational problems. Many books today use a word to label a problem that might be responsible for why some individuals never marry. That word is "commitmentphobia." Some experts suggest this problem has reached epidemic proportions. It's especially painful for the person who deeply loves a partner who cannot bring himself or herself to make a commitment. Numerous books discuss this problem, and usually men are the culprits. A few titles are *The Dance-Away Lover, The Go-Away-Come-Closer Disease, The Playboy Syndrome, Flight from Commitment, The Peter Pan Syndrome,* and *Men Who Can't Love.*

A "commitmentphobic" is a person who has a strong, insatiable desire for affirmation from the opposite sex as well as a resistance to commitment. Commitmentphobics don't want to be alone, but they don't want to be too close either. When they do get too close, they retreat. Their double message

A "commitment-phobic" is a person who has a strong, insatiable desire for affirmation from the opposite sex as well as a resistance to commitment.

is, "Come closer. Don't get too close. Come here. Go away."
They're unhappy by themselves and unhappy if they're
going to be tied down.

How do you detect commitmentphobics? If he has a
history of short-term relationships, beware. Does she
cancel dates with you or change arrangements frequently? Do you find yourself being hurt by him? Do
you see her settling down and changing her patterns? If
not, be careful.

If for some reason you have a strong feeling you're
involved with such a person, get out. Don't try to discover
why he or she is like this. Don't try and change the individual. You won't and you can't. It's easy to fall into the trap of
"I wonder why she canceled again?" or "I wonder why he's
retreating?" You probably will never find out. Move on to
someone with potential.

Another frequent cause for concern among women is
committed bachelors. A newspaper carried an article
titled "Bachelor Fad," which stated more and more men
are choosing the single life rather than marriage. Although
many men postpone marriage to pursue educational and
career goals, the author of the book *Bachelors: The Psy-
chology of Never-Married Men* found that many men never
marry because it is their choice not to do so. The author's
study revealed that many men have three types of defenses
in relationships: avoidance, isolation, and distortion.

These single men appeared reluctant to become involved emotionally or share their needs. Their defensiveness and isolation made it impossible for them to relate
to women on anything but a superficial level. Overall their
tendency was to be standoffish and indifferent. If there
were any situations in which they might be hurt, they
avoided the situation. One of the more striking points of
the study is that it revealed only 5 percent of bachelors
over forty ever marry![1]

Obsessive Love

In a healthy relationship you may hope you have found the person who will be the fulfillment of your hopes and dreams. But usually this hope is balanced with the realistic knowledge that it may not work out. You have a safety net called reality. An obsessive lover works without a net and won't even consider the possibility of a breakup. When this person finds a new partner, he or she cries out, "Yes! This is my magic person who can meet all my needs and give me happiness." The fantastical expectations of a person obsessed with love have very little to do with who the other person really is. The focus is on what he or she needs and how the other person can meet those needs.[2]

The obsessive lover often has a consuming, intense, even painful preoccupation for a certain individual. He or she is consumed by either possessing this person or being possessed by him or her. The pursued person is often unavailable in some way or may have already rejected the obsessive lover. But it doesn't matter; the rejection actually feeds the obsession. Because of the unavailability or rejection, the obsessive lover begins to behave in self-defeating ways.[3] Statements like the following are common:

"I know she dates other men, but they really aren't significant to her. She really cares only for me. She'll realize that soon."

"I call him several times a day and he hangs up. He just can't face how much he cares for me. I guess he's overwhelmed by it and can't handle it. Someday he will."

"He hasn't called for two weeks. It's happened before when work gets really busy. When it lets up, he'll be back."

All these statements deny the truth.

When sex is a part of this kind of relationship, it further clutters things. And in most obsessive relationships, sex plays a major role. The sex is usually very intense and pleasurable, but the problem is that it's used to measure the intensity of love and compatibility, which leads to idealization of the other person. The obsessive person takes the sexual interaction to mean that this relationship is "the one"—a sure sign that sex has been mistaken for love—and the short-term passion makes the eventual rejection hurt even more.

As I have worked with couples in premarital counseling over the years, I've found about half of them have a pure sexual relationship. They are not having, nor have they had, sexual intercourse. I ask counselees who are engaged in sexual activity to bring this to a halt and to maintain a pure sexual relationship until the wedding night. They agree to this, and in time many of them make a decision not to marry. Why? Several have said, including men, that when the sex stopped, they could see their problems more clearly and the driving passion that kept them together dissipated.

An individual can overcome an obsessive love difficulty. If you or someone you are seeing has this problem, put all involvement and dating on hold until it is resolved. It can lead to obsessive pursuit, revenge, stalking, and even violence. An obsession with love can have the following charactestics, and it only takes a few of these to indicate a problem:

The obsessed pursuer yearns for a person who isn't physically or emotionally available to him or her.

The obsessed pursuer lives for the time when his or her desired one will be available.

The obsessed pursuer believes that if he or she wants the other enough, eventually the other will have to love him or her.

161

When the obsessed pursuer is rejected, he or she wants the other even more, and continued rejections lead to depression or rage.

The obsessed pursuer feels victimized because of the lack of response on the part of the other individual.

The obsessed pursuer believes only this one person can fulfill his or her life.

The obsessed pursuer is so preoccupied with the other individual that his or her work, eating, and sleeping habits are affected.

The obsessed pursuer calls the person constantly, watches and checks up on him or her, and so on.[4]

This may sound sick to you. It is. But it is reversible; the person can develop normal and healthy relationships.[5]

More Problems to Avoid

Years ago I read a book called *The Givers and the Takers*. As the title suggests, it divided people into one of two camps. Ideally we have the ability to both give and receive, but if your partner is exclusively one or the other, you can count on one thing: your needs won't be met. Consider the potential of a relationship where either you or your partner is the one who's always giving.

If your partner uses threats of any kind to force you to continue to be involved with him or her, such as violence, ruining your reputation, or suicide, you need to end the relationship as soon as possible. Get out.

I'm amazed at the number of married Christian couples who use the "D" word as a threat to control each other. If you have a partner who uses threats to get his or her way, you might consider showing him or her the door!

Don't spend time pursuing someone with an *addiction*. You'll lose because whatever the addiction is, it's your rival and the other person is its slave. It doesn't matter whether it's alcohol, pornography, drugs, or food, all addictions are equally destructive. And if the person you're considering is in recovery, how long has it been and what's his or her track record?

Don't get involved with a habitually angry person. Scripture says, "Make no friendships with a man given to anger, and with a wrathful man do not associate, lest you learn his ways and get yourself into a snare" (Prov. 22:24–25 AMP). Don't put up with anger. Don't think you can fix a person who's always raging. The last thing a person needs is to be an object of someone else's emotional abuse.

Have you ever been involved with someone who has a habit of acting like a victim? Such people blame others for their problems, complain incessantly, and won't take responsibility for their own actions. For them, life stinks. They see themselves as helpless and powerless, and they're likely to be passive-aggressive. How would you like to be married to a person like this? Stay away from self-proclaiming victims.

One of the saddest sights I've ever seen is an adult who hasn't grown up. There are three words to describe this person: irresponsible (especially financially), undependable (late, forgetful, breaks promises, etc.), and unmotivated. These behaviors aren't cute. They're a violation of Scripture and shouldn't be tolerated.

Have you ever dated someone whom you tried to get close to, yet every time you took a step closer, he or she took a step away? If the other person has "no emotional trespassing" signs posted, don't go there. You don't need a partner who is emotionally unavailable. After all, the purpose of a relationship is emotional connection, so don't

163

bother. If they can't or won't show or talk about emotions, can't open up and don't want to learn how to, forget about them. Just remember, if you marry someone like this, you won't have a relationship; you'll have a living arrangement.

There's one more problem, and it has to do with baggage. Some years ago my wife and I had an opportunity to take a cruise on a large ocean liner. Since our itinerary and calendar had been selected for us in advance, our main concern was selecting what we would take with us. As we looked at the pile of stuff strewn on the living room floor, it was hard to believe this voyage was to last only eight days. It looked more like a scene from *Around the World in 80 Days*! We knew that if we were not careful in selecting what we should take with us, we would end up with an incredible amount of excess baggage.

So we began to sort through the pile and ask, Do we really need this item? Will I ever wear this outfit? However, even with careful selecting we still took too much. On board, we unpacked and hung as much as we could in the closet, but we had brought too many clothes, and they wouldn't fit even if we crammed them in. We went through a selecting process *again* and put some of our belongings back in the suitcases and boxes. We then stashed some of our bags under the bed, out of the way. That worked during the day, but when we wanted to rest or sleep, the bulge in the bed kept us from being as comfortable as we could have been. You get the picture. We both decided that if we ever had it to do again, we would be more selective.

Just as my wife and I carried excess baggage on our trip, we may drag along excess luggage on our trip through life. We all start out at birth and sail ahead into childhood, adolescence, and on to adulthood, collecting baggage. And this baggage—the influences and pressures from our parents and other people in our childhood—has a significant bearing upon our adult life. We are supposed to move out of childhood and become an adult, but the fact is we hang on to much of the excess baggage of our childhood.

Everyone has some carryover "stuff" from childhood, but the question is, To what extent is there *emotional damage?* It's amazing to discover how many people come from backgrounds with sexual, physical, or emotional abuse; parental abandonment of some kind; eating disorders; or parental addictions.

Three questions will help you put these issues in perspective as they relate to a potential partner:

How severe was the damage when this person was young?

Is he or she aware of the damage and its impact on a relationship?

Is he or she working on repairing this damage?

The good news is I've seen many who are not only survivors of childhood abuse but are also in healthy relationships. But the answers to the above three questions are critical.

I've addressed these issues as they pertain to someone you're considering for a relationship. But it's just as important that you look at your own life in regard to these issues and ask, "Do any of these describe me and if so, what do I need to do about it?" The good news is change *is* possible, especially if you know Jesus Christ as your Savior.[6]

Right now let's do some work that will improve your relationships in the future. We can allow our past to dominate our present and future, or we can take charge of our past and learn from it in order to change the future.

Some of the following questions have the potential of activating feelings of loss and pain. They also might prompt you to berate and kick yourself with statements like, "I

165

should have known. Why was I so blind?" or "What's wrong with me?" I encourage you to focus on what you will do differently the next time around. If your answer to a question is not what you would like it to be, decide to act differently the next time around.

Do you have a pattern of involvement with those who seem to avoid commitment?

Do you spend time fantasizing about relationships including the ideal person or past persons?

Do you find yourself attracted to those who would be poor partners?

Do you ever find yourself more committed to the potential of the relationship than the person?

When you have a relationship, are you more interested and committed when they're elsewhere than when you're together?

Are you attracted more to stable, reliable individuals or to more exciting and less stable types?

Are you attracted to the challenge of making changes and corrections in a partner when changes are needed?

In the past, when relationships have ended, did your grief response

a. end in a couple of weeks?

b. seem to go on forever or until a new partner was discovered?

c. not exist?

d. go on for an appropriate amount of time, and you recovered before seeking a new relationship?

Do you put yourself in appropriate places to meet others?

Have you ever continued a relationship even though you knew right from the start it would never last (because, after all, a poor relationship is better than none at all)?[7]

Below is some space for you to list five things you'll do differently in your next relationship:

1.
2.
3.
4.
5.

The Nature of Problems

I've seen some strange situations in premarital counseling. I've talked with engaged couples where one partner didn't especially like the other but felt attraction wasn't necessary if physical needs were met. Another couple admitted they had a physical attraction to one another and had similar goals financially, but they were not sure they liked each other's personality! Why would people even consider marriage with these liabilities? Yet they do. Fortunately, the couples I mentioned eventually decided not to marry.

Think about the numerous problems already mentioned in this chapter in this way: if there is an issue now, why wouldn't it be a problem after marriage, with even greater intensity? If you can take the necessary steps to resolve such issues as those mentioned in this chapter, great, but realize it's going to take time.[8]

Why do so many people stay in relationships that are laden with warning signals? It could be because of low self-esteem. One forty-year-old counselee described her dilemma with her boyfriend. She told me about his constant put-downs, which made her self-esteem crumble. I asked why she didn't end the relationship, and she said, "I would miss out on the companionship I have. I'd be uncomfortable starting over with someone else. And maybe his negative perceptions of me are accurate." Her statement goes to show you that if you hear negatives enough, you begin to believe them.

Some individuals seem to be ruled by their feelings regardless of the objective facts. I see many people who spend their time in romance novels and otherwise feeding their fantasies. Sometimes what you fantasize about becomes so intense that it can override reality, and you fail to notice danger signals.

12

Creating a Healthy Relationship

Every relationship we have is either a *depleting* or a *replenishing* relationship. A depleting relationship is one in which you are with someone who drains you emotionally and spiritually. The relationship taps your energy reserves in some way. It can happen in long-term dating relationships or in a marriage. Being around this type of person is just plain hard work. At first the relationship may seem workable, but soon it becomes an exercise in coping. Those who deplete you contribute to your problems rather than help you resolve them.

You don't want a depleting relationship—in any kind of situation. You want replenishing relationships—relationships with people who energize and vitalize you. They add to your life in a positive way. And one of the best ways to draw people like this is to be this kind of person yourself.[1]

By Choice or by Force

Think back to your last relationship. Were you in the relationship because you clearly chose to be, or did you feel you "had" to be with that person? Consider a friend of mine, June. She's in a relationship with and is really drawn to Tim. She's willing to make sacrifices to make the relationship work. She's given to the relationship but still maintains her objectivity. An important factor is that *her judgment controls her emotions,* so she's in charge of her choices. She expects to be treated properly and with respect. She holds Tim accountable for his actions as he does the same for her.

My other friend Sue, on the other hand, had been dating Richard for several months. He tended to take her for granted in many ways. He was a taker, and Sue found herself giving more and more. The more she gave and tried, the emptier she felt—especially because Richard didn't get the message that he should be a giver himself.

Although others suggested to Sue that she could do better and needed to move on, she believed if she tried harder, the relationship would improve and, of course, that Richard would change. But the longer she stayed in the relationship, the more she felt controlled by it. It's as though she thought she was making choices, but the reality is that *the relationship took over.* Her freedom of choice seemed to be crippled. After several months the relationship failed.

These two patterns can exist whether you're male or female. If you freely *choose* to be with someone, it's healthy. If you are *driven* or *compelled* to be with someone, it's unhealthy.

Fixers and Givers

A healthy relationship is characterized by mutual strength, support, and equality—you help each other grow, to be the best you can be. In a healthy relationship each participant acts as a cheerleader or encourager to the other. They help each other by being involved in each other's ups and downs.

An unhealthy relationship often contains a "fixer." One person takes it upon himself or herself to reform, restructure, or even fix the other person. The relationship is off-balance. It's tilted, and the more something tilts, the greater is its instability. One individual has an abundance of needs, whereas the other needs to be needed. The fixer seems to thrive on helping and being needed. But this only serves to perpetuate the problem. Both members take action when they should let go; yet when they really should do something, they fail to take the proper steps. They become caretakers, doing for the other person what that person is capable of doing for him- or herself.

In a healthy relationship each participant acts as a cheerleader or encourager to the other.

There's another pattern very similar to this one. It's a pattern I've seen in many unhealthy relationships over the years, and I'd like to illustrate it with something I did once. One day I took a carton of milk out of the refrigerator, turned around to the counter, and began to pour it into a glass that I thought I had placed there. The milk went everywhere, and while my two golden retrievers appreciated it, it did nothing for me. The milk needed to be poured into something with structure, with boundaries. In an unhealthy relationship, there is often a person who pours himself or herself out

171

for their partner. One is a giver, the other a taker. But that's not the way a relationship is supposed to work. When we enter a relationship, we are not supposed to lose our individual sense of who we are. Listed below are some traits of unhealthy boundaries. Look back at your last relationship and evaluate yourself on a scale from 0 to 10 for each one, 0 meaning the trait most certainly did not apply and 10 meaning it most certainly did. Drawing a circle or a box respectively, evaluate where you were as well as where your former partner was:

Found it difficult to keep confidences and secrets.

0 1 2 3 4 5 6 7 8 9 10

Revealed too much on an intimate level too soon.

0 1 2 3 4 5 6 7 8 9 10

Fell in love at first sight.

0 1 2 3 4 5 6 7 8 9 10

Responded with love to anyone who showed interest.

0 1 2 3 4 5 6 7 8 9 10

Thought about the other person all the time.

0 1 2 3 4 5 6 7 8 9 10

Went against personal standards of sexual behavior.

0 1 2 3 4 5 6 7 8 9 10

Accepted gifts, food, or touching that were not wanted.

0 1 2 3 4 5 6 7 8 9 10

Believed that his or her (or your) own opinion did not matter.

0 1 2 3 4 5 6 7 8 9 10

Was always "doing" for the other.

0 1 2 3 4 5 6 7 8 9 10

Let others make decisions for him or her (or you).

0　1　2　3　4　5　6　7　8　9　10

Let others dictate how to feel.

0　1　2　3　4　5　6　7　8　9　10

Let the other decide who to relate to and be friends with.

0　1　2　3　4　5　6　7　8　9　10

Tolerated any kind of abuse whether emotional, physical, or sexual.

0　1　2　3　4　5　6　7　8　9　10

Felt obligated to do things for strangers.

0　1　2　3　4　5　6　7　8　9　10

Had a difficult time saying no.

0　1　2　3　4　5　6　7　8　9　10

How do you see yourself now? Are you satisfied with where you are? What about your past partner? What did you learn about this person from this exercise?

Objectivity vs. Blind Love

In healthy relationships one person is objective about the other person rather than being blind to his or her faults. If your relationship was healthy, you recognized strengths and faults in both yourself and your partner. You were able to see shortcomings and areas in which you needed to grow.

Believe it or not, there are relationships in which love really is blind. One partner sees the other almost as a demigod. He or she can do no wrong. Faults are nonexistent because they are denied or overlooked.

If the other person is perfect, what happens to the need for growth? This isn't love, it's infatuation. Infatuation is like a giant balloon that blinds someone from seeing who the other really is. One day the balloon bursts, and the formerly infatuated individual is left astonished at all the flaws of his or her partner.

Honesty vs. Criticism

Honesty must be an ingredient in your relationship; however, there are distinct differences between honesty and criticism. Honesty is sharing truth and feelings in a straightforward fashion, in a way that grows out of fairness and respect. It means being frank, but with tact and sensitivity.

Criticism, however, means you make judgments, find faults, and show disapproval because others don't respond or say things in the way you want. It's saying, "My way is the best and *only* way to do something; if you don't do things my way, you're wrong and deficient."

Look at the following differences between honesty and criticism, compiled by the authors of *Two Friends in Love*:

Honesty can hurt, but criticism always injures.

Honesty brings healing, but criticism promotes pain.

Honesty is shared with open hands; criticism contains a pointing, accusing finger.

Honesty is straightforward; criticism involves game-playing.

Honesty wants the good for both of you whereas criticism wants good for the critic.

Honesty is built on facts and principles; criticism builds on assumptions and unrealistic assumptions.

Honesty is unselfish; criticism wants only what it wants.

With honesty, you both win. With criticism, you both lose.[2]

Time Together vs. Time with Others

Another area of concern has to do with balance between attention to one's partner and interaction with other friends. When two people begin a romantic relationship, they often want to spend more time with each other and less time with others. This is normal and natural. People in a relationship tend to alter their schedules to some extent. In a healthy relationship, you know you have priority in each other's life, but you don't live exclusively for each other. Some of your needs are met by others outside the relationship. If your relationship is healthy, longtime friendships won't be a threat.

But when all your time and attention are eaten up by the other person, you'll feel confined and controlled. Your romantic interest cannot meet all of your needs, no matter how hard you or your partner tries. Friends should continue to meet some of your recreational, social, or intellectual needs. A relationship is not supposed to be an imprisonment, either self-imposed or other-imposed. If it becomes an imprisonment, eventually there will be a jailbreak!

A relationship is not supposed to be an imprisonment, either self-imposed or other-imposed.

A healthy relationship makes you a stronger person, both when you're with your partner and when you're not. In a good relationship, you feel good about yourself and the relationship when you're apart. In an unhealthy relationship, you may experience a high when you're together, but a major letdown when you're apart.[3]

Trust vs. Jealousy

Healthy relationships have a high degree of trust. You believe in the other person to do the right thing. You take

175

him at his word. You give her the benefit of the doubt. You don't make negative assumptions about your partner. If you do make assumptions, they're positive. The opposite of a relationship of trust is a relationship of jealousy. Listen to the following information about jealousy:

> Jealousy is an ugly monster. It can take over a relationship and destroy it. Jealousy is born of insecurity and desire. It is not known to be reasonable. Wild charges are made, exposing deep feelings of pain or fear. If you have been jealous within a relationship, you know how it gnaws at you, defying your attempts to control it. If your partner has been the jealous one, you know how frustrating it can be to sidestep the traps that monster sets.
>
> The jealous person fears that the partner will leave for someone more physically attractive, more interesting, more suitable, or more financially stable. This possibility creates panic and results in irrational attempts to control the partner's life. This reaction can chase the partner away unless the partner is addicted, too.[4]

Jealousy usually begins with possessiveness, which is dangerous. It pushes the other person away. In your last relationship, to what degree did you tend to be a trusting person? To what degree did your previous partner tend to be a trusting person? To what degree did you tend to be a jealous person? To what degree did your previous partner tend to be a jealous person?

Taking Risks vs. Stuck in a Rut

A healthy relationship contains two individuals (not just one) who are open to change, rather than clinging to unhealthy patterns from the past. Those who are open to change have more opportunity to operate or function as they should.

The authors of *Love Gone Wrong* give a good analogy of the difference between being functional and dysfunctional:

> When I'm driving my car, I have a problem if I have a flat tire. I might even consider it a crisis. And I could probably call it a *misfunction*. The tire, being flat, isn't doing what a tire should do. I stop and fix it and drive on.
>
> But if my car is badly out of alignment, that's another thing. It affects my steering, the car wobbles to the right as I drive, and my tires get worn quickly on one side, leading to more flat tires. It might be considered a *dysfunction*. It's not just when one thing goes wrong. It's when the whole system goes out of whack.[5]

To be functional, you have to risk. To move ahead, you have to risk. To find what is worthwhile in life, you have to risk. To risk means giving up some security (though some of what we call security is actually false security) for the sake of growing and moving forward.

There is a twenty-five-mile stretch of highway in the high desert area of southern California that I travel once or twice a year. It's not my favorite stretch of road because it has only two lanes and the frequent dips tend to hide oncoming cars. When I'm stuck behind a slow-plodding driver, I have the choice of staying behind him or looking for an opportunity to pass. When I think about passing, I must not only observe the slow vehicle I'm following but watch for oncoming traffic. Then I have to determine if there is enough highway between me and the approaching cars to allow me to pass.

When passing, these are the steps involved: preparing adequately, making a commitment, and then following through by pressing the accelerator to the floor and surging around the slower driver and moving back into the right lane. Most people succeed in passing with minimal anxiety when they follow these steps. But the driver who hesitates when he pulls out into the left lane adds stress to the situation and is a danger to himself.

Similarly, when we risk and choose to change in the area of personal growth, we must be committed to follow through. I would rather choose to take a risk than be forced to take one. Which would you prefer? If we postpone taking risks when they are needed, we may be forced to accept something we don't want, or to take risks when we are least prepared for them.

Remember: In unhealthy relationships people bind themselves to the past and refuse to change and grow. In healthy relationships people are determined to let go of self-defeating patterns and move on.

Good Fights vs. Bad Fights

A healthy relationship moves conflicts toward resolution and uses disagreement as a means to growth. No relationship is totally without conflict. In healthy relationships the partners are determined to resolve conflicts, to make each conflict a means of growth. Unhealthy relationships often develop into love-hate relationships.

Some relationships just move from one unresolved conflict to another. I've seen couples in marital counseling who come in and say, "It's not that we don't talk about our issues. We've been talking about them for twenty years. We just don't resolve them." They have never learned necessary problem-solving skills.

Many unhealthy relationships are characterized by avoidance. The partners do not talk about the issues; they bury them. In time, however, the hot issues smolder and eventually create an emotional explosion that could last for days. Then once again there's calm. It's a repetitive cycle.

Remember that the definition of a conflict is nothing more than a difference in point of view. Many conflicts have to do with the distance or lack thereof between two people. People fight with one another when they want distance and when they want closeness. Conflict can accomplish several things. It can lead to a discovery of truth. It can stretch our perspectives, enabling us to consider more than one point of view. It can help us change our patterns of communication. Conflict helps us learn what works and what doesn't. It opens up blocked lines of communication. In these ways we can become solution-oriented instead of problem-oriented people.[6]

Conclusion

As you've read through these issues, I'm sure it was natural for you to think about previous relationships. If the information in this chapter helped you to see issues and problems in your past relationships, there are some steps you can take that will help future relationships.

The first thing you can do is define what you want and what you need from a relationship. Be specific and describe it in writing. Then identify precisely what you are willing to give to a new relationship. If you have a trusted group of good friends or an older mentor-type couple, discuss this with them and listen closely to their feedback.

Some couples create an agreed-upon set of rules and guidelines, which might include items like the following:

the amount of time you want to spend together

the amount of time you want to spend with others

who will do what for whom

no critical comments in public

call if you're running late[7]

Before you enter a new relationship, be sure to use the form titled *Preparing for a New Relationship,* found in the appendix.

179

Appendix

Preparing for a New Relationship

(Permission granted to make a single photocopy of this section for your partner.)

A. Describe your expectations for your next relationship.

_____

_____

_____

_____

_____

_____

_____

_____

B. What was your last relationship like? Let's compare it with your new prospective partner.

1. How long did you know your previous partner before you began to date?

   _____

   _____

   How long did you know your current partner before you began to date?

   _____

   _____

2. What attracted you to your former?

   _____

   _____

   _____

   What attracts you to your current?

   _____

   _____

   _____

3. What dream did you have for your prior relationship?

   _____

   _____

   _____

   _____

   _____

   _____

What dream do you have for this relationship?

_____

_____

_____

_____

_____

_____

_____

C. Characteristics and personality traits.

1. List ten adjectives that describe your former partner.

1. _____ 6. _____
2. _____ 7. _____
3. _____ 8. _____
4. _____ 9. _____
5. _____ 10. _____

2. What do you know about the prospective person? List as many adjectives as you can describing this person.

1. _____ 6. _____
2. _____ 7. _____
3. _____ 8. _____
4. _____ 9. _____
5. _____ 10. _____

Now indicate with a check mark the adjectives in both lists that describe you.

3. Underline any of the following descriptions that apply to you. Place a check mark by any that apply to the person in your last relationship. Circle any that apply to the person in your prospective relationship.

Perfectionistic tendencies	Use of pornography
Overworks	Loss of control
Sleeps too much	Worry
Compulsive behavior	Use of drugs
Procrastination	Depression
Difficulty at work	Aggressive behavior
Type A behavior	Use of alcohol
Smokes	Low self-esteem
Insomnia	Overeats
Risk taker	Withdraws from others
Suicidal threats	Verbally abusive
Crying	Physicallyabusive
Impulsive behavior	Lazy
Suicidal behavior	

4. Below is a graph to help you see when your level of satisfaction with your relationship began to falter and then fail. On the bottom line of the graph fill in time increments, such as "1 month," "2 months," and so on, or "2 months," "4 months," and so on, depending on how long you were in the relationship. Then make a dot above each time increment, indicating your satisfaction level.

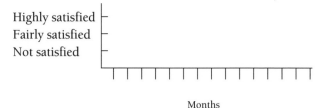

Highly satisfied
Fairly satisfied
Not satisfied

Months

184

What did you do to improve the relationship?

_____

_____

_____

_____

_____

_____

Describe in detail how your breakup has impacted and changed you.

_____

_____

_____

_____

_____

_____

What will you bring into this next relationship from the previous one?

_____

_____

_____

_____

_____

_____

What do you *not* want to bring to your next relationship and how will you avoid this?

_____

_____

_____

_____

_____

_____

5. Describe the pattern of satisfaction you predict you will have in your new relationship.

Highly satisfied

Fairly satisfied

Not satisfied

Months

Now describe specifically what you will do to make this a reality.

_____

_____

_____

_____

_____

6. In what ways is your present relationship similar to the former one?

_____

_____

_____

_____

_____

7. In what ways is your present relationship different from the former one?

_____

_____

_____

_____

_____

Notes

Chapter 1

1. Carolyn N. Bushong, *Seven Dumbest Relationship Mistakes Smart People Make* (New York: Villard Books, 1997), 152–172.

2. Miriam Elliot and Susan Mettzer, *The Perfectionist Predicament* (New York: William Morrow and Co., 1991), 262–263.

3. H. Norman Wright, *Relationships That Work & Those That Don't* (Ventura, Calif.: Regal Books, 1998), 115–127.

4. Dr. Bonnie Eaker Weil, with Toni Robino, *Make Up, Don't Break Up* (Holbrook, Mass.: Adams Media Co., 1999), 186–189.

5. Ibid., 12–19.

6. Ibid., 192.

7. Steven Carter and Julia Sokol, *He's Scared, She's Scared* (New York: Dell, 1993), 128.

8. Shmuley Boteach, *Dating Secrets of the Ten Commandments* (New York: Doubleday, 2000), 139–140. Used by permission.

Chapter 2

1. Margaret Kent, *How to Marry the Man of Your Choice* (New York: Warner Books, 1984), 284.

2. Jim Smoke, *Growing in Remarriage* (Old Tappan, N.J.: Fleming H. Revell, 1990), 47.

3. Neil Clark Warren, *Ten Dates or Less* (Nashville: Thomas Nelson, 1999), 75–85.

4. Ibid., 98–107.

Chapter 3

1. Roseanne Rosen, *The Complete Idiot's Guide to Handling a Breakup* (New York: Alpha Publishing, 1999), 70.

2. Carter and Sokol, *He's Scared, She's Scared*, 272–284.

3. Rosen, *The Complete Idiot's Guide*, 67–68.

4. Ibid., 71.

5. Smoke, *Growing in Remarriage*, 193–210.

6. Henry Cloud and John Townsend, *Boundaries in Dating* (Grand Rapids: Zondervan, 2000), 234, 236.

Chapter 4

1. Chuck Spezzano, *Heal Your Heartbreak* (New York: Marlowe & Co., 2000), 100, 148.

2. Zev Wanderer and Tracy Cobot, *Letting Go* (New York: Dell Books, 1978), 11–12.

3. Stephen Gullo and Connie Church, *Love Shock: How to Recover from a Broken Heart and Live Again* (New York: Bantam Books, 1988), 26.

4. Diane Vaughan, *Uncoupling* (New York: Oxford University Press, 1986), 140–147.

5. Ibid., 42–43.

Chapter 5

1. Dick Innes, *How to Mend a Broken Heart* (Grand Rapids: Baker Book House, 1994), 36.

2. Rosen, *The Complete Idiot's Guide*, 180.

3. Henri J. M. Nouwen, *The Living Reminder: Service and Prayer in Memory of Jesus Christ* (New York: Seabury Press, 1977), 19.

4. Ibid., 22.

5. Scott M. Stanley, *The Heart of Commitment* (Nashville: Thomas Nelson, 1998), 80–88.

6. Therese A. Rando, *Grieving: How to Go On Living When Someone You Love Dies* (Lexington, Mass.: Lexington Books, 1988), 11–12.

7. Innes, *How to Mend a Broken Heart*, 42–43.

8. Ibid., 47.

9. Rando, *Grieving*, 18–19.

10. Bob Diets, *Life after Loss* (Tucson: Fisher Books, 1988), 27.

Chapter 6

1. Billy Sprague, *Letter to a Grieving Heart* (Eugene, Ore.: Harvest House, 2001), 9, 39.

2. Wanderer and Cabot, *Letting Go*, 27–28.

3. Ibid., 38–39.

4. Gary Emery, *A New Beginning: How You Can Change Your Thoughts through Cognitive Therapy* (New York: Simon & Schuster, 1981, 1988), 61, table.

5. Wanderer and Cabot, *Letting Go*, 97–100.

Chapter 7

1. Thomas Whiteman and Randy Petersen, *Fresh Start: 8 Principles for Starting Over When a Relationship Doesn't Work* (Wheaton, Ill.: Tyndale, 1997), 125–129.

2. Lewis B. Smedes, "Forgiveness, the Power to Change the Past," *Christianity Today*, 7 January 1983, 26.

3. Lewis B. Smedes, *Forgive and Forget* (New York: Harper and Row, 1984), 37.

4. Scott Nelson, *Lost Lovers, Found Friends* (New York: Simon & Schuster, 1991), 58.

5. Ibid., 84.

6. Wanderer and Cabot, *Letting Go*, 68–71, 156–165.

7. H. Norman Wright, *Finding Your Perfect Mate* (Eugene, Ore.: Harvest House, 1995), chapter 3.

Chapter 8

1. Ann Kaiser Stearns, *Living through Personal Crisis* (Chicago: Thomas Moore, 1984), 85–86.

2. Aleta Koman, *How to Mend a Broken Heart* (Chicago: Contemporary Books, 1997), 174–182.

3. Dwight Carlson, *When Life Isn't Fair* (Eugene, Ore.: Harvest House Publishers, 1989), 38.

4. Ibid., 43.

5. Whiteman and Petersen, *Fresh Start*, 83–84.

6. Ibid., 100–103.

7. Ibid., 113–115.

8. Carter and Sokol, *He's Scared, She's Scared*, 172–174.

Chapter 9

1. Linda Rich, "No One" (poem, 1970), assigned to InterVarsity Christian Fellowship of the USA.

2. John Ortberg, *If You Want to Walk on Water, You Have to Get Out of the Boat* (Grand Rapids: Zondervan, 2000), 180–181. Used by permission.

3. Jacqueline Olds, Richard Schwartz, and Harriet Webster, *Overcoming Loneliness in Everyday Life* (New York: Carol Pub. Group, 1996), 119–120.

4. Cloud and Townsend, *Boundaries in Dating*, 73.

5. Ibid., 74.

6. Ibid., 74–75.

7. Dick Purnell, *Becoming a Friend and Lover* (Nashville: Thomas Nelson, 1995), 242.

8. Ibid., 242–243.

9. Tim Stafford, *A Love Story* (Grand Rapids: Zondervan Publishing, 1977), 91–93.

Chapter 10

1. Gary Rosburg, *Guard Your Heart* (Sisters, Ore.: Multnomah, 1994), 15–17.

2. Robbie Castleman, *True Love* (Downer's Grove, Ill.: InterVarsity Press, 1996), 45–46.

3. Michael S. Broder, *The Art of Staying Together* (New York: Hyperion, 1993), 25–26.

4. Tina Tessins, *The Unofficial Guide to Dating* (New York: MacMillan, 1998), 28–48.

5. Boteach, *Dating Secrets*, 45. Used by permission.

6. Broder, *The Art of Staying Together*, 128.

7. Carter and Sokol, *He's Scared, She's Scared*, 18–29.

8. Rebecca Cutter, *When Opposites Attract: Right Brain/Left Brain Relationships and How to Make Them Work* (New York: Dutton, 1994), 149–150.

Chapter 11

1. Darryl E. Owens, "Bachelor Fad," *The Orlando Sentinel*, in *Missoulian*, 20 June 1994.

2. Dr. Susan Forward, *Obsessive Love* (New York: Bantam Books, 1991), 22–24.

3. Ibid., 7.

4. Ibid., 11–12.

5. Wright, *Finding Your Perfect Mate*, 136–148.

6. Barbara De Angelis, *Are You the One for Me?* (New York: Dell Publishing, 1992), 160–205.

7. Carter and Sokol, *He's Scared, She's Scared*, 170.

8. Michael S. Broder, *The Art of Staying Together* (New York: MacMillan, 1998), 127–131.

Chapter 12

1. Ronnie W. Floyd, *Choices* (Nashville: Broadman and Holman, 1994), 70–74.

2. Ed and Carol Newenschwander, *Two Friends in Love* (Sisters, Ore.: Multnomah, 1986), 154–155.

3. Whiteman and Petersen, *Fresh Start,* 34–36.

4. Thomas A. Whiteman and Randy Petersen, *Love Gone Wrong* (Nashville: Thomas Nelson, 1994), 46.

5. Ibid., 49–50.

6. Dave and Jan Congo, *The Power of Love* (Chicago: Moody Press, 1993), 70.

7. Wright, *Relationships That Work & Those That Don't,* 16–17, 99–111.

H. Norman Wright is the author of more than sixty books and a household name among Christian booksellers. He is a licensed marriage, family, and child therapist, and has taught undergraduate and graduate level classes, as well as seminars at many colleges and seminaries. The founder and director of Christian Marriage Enrichment, he lives with his wife, Joyce, in California.